For all you Ro
Casanovas and 1
gigolettes, all you si
à trois. For all you
you wooers and wooees, for all who've ever been
touched by Cupid's dart, here's the ultimate
guide to

Dating, Mating, Relating

*This is your guide to Romantic Love, Puppy
Love, Platonic Love, and the naughty kind,
too: where to get it, how to keep it, how to lose
it, and where to get more. From opening lines
to parting shots; the myths, the math, the
magic of . . .*

The Big L.

Dating, Mating, Relating

written and illustrated by
David Westwood

LONGMEADOW
P R E S S

Thanks to
John Berley, Charles Frewin,
Jo Glorie, Laurie Goodman,
Derek Lubner, Jerry Leibowitz,
Scott Wyant

"The Relationship" originally appeared, in revised form, in *New Woman* and is reprinted here with permission.

Cover design by Richard Oriolo

Interior design by Richard Oriolo

ISBN: 0-681-00773-7

Printed in U.S.A.

First U.S.A. Edition

0 9 8 7 6 5 4 3 2 1

Contents

I. Dating

II. Mating

III. Relating

I

Dating

1: Blind-Date Types

If I wanted to shorten my life I'd date you, but I was hoping for something higher up on the food chain.

—Judy Tenuta

Be prepared. Decipher those descriptions when dating agencies or your so-called friends try to set you up.

ambitious: mercenary; will go out with you as long as you can advance their career, do their laundry, or fix their car.

assertive: angry, hostile, bitter and twisted, and looking for a sucker to dump it all on.

available: on the rebound.

brilliant: boring.

bubbly: brains have been carbonated.

complex: schizophrenic.

confirmed bachelor: hasn't done his dishes in twelve years; refrigerator contains ten six-packs of Heineken, a quart of Haägen-Dazs Rum Raisin, a Tupperware container that's been there so long he's afraid to open it, and various round things covered in blue fur.

cute: for men: has long eyelashes, dimples; for women: doll-like, wears children's clothing, talks as if she has a mouth full of helium.

deep: incomprehensible, apt to ramble on about Keats or Kierkegaard. See **poetic**.

diamond in the rough: undersocialized; wipes nose on sleeve; has a tendency to drink out of the toilet every now and then. Not the kind of person to take home for Thanksgiving, unless it's at the homeless shelter.

earth mother: always in the kitchen baking something, wears voluminous dresses, good for a foot rub.

earthy: crass, crude, primitive; lends proof to the theory that the Neanderthal did not necessarily die out. See **diamond in the rough**.

elegant/willowy: anorexic, emaciated, better with clothes *on*.

ethnic-looking: has a macawlike nose.

experienced: a. middle-aged, been married eight times b. an ex-addict.

feisty: makes every decision into an argument; running for mayor.

frigid: she wouldn't go to bed with me.

full-figured/ample/cuddly: built to last, industrial strength.

handsome: one of those double-standard words. For men: good looking; for women: trucklike. See **pretty**.

has a good job: boring.

has a great inner beauty: has a great outer ugliness.

has character: has the personality of a sowbug.

has great personality: has looks that would make a train take a dirt road; has no character.

imaginative
a. paranoid
b. a compulsive liar.

intense: Mansonesque; has seen *Silence of the Lambs* ten times, talks about some people "having the Devil inside them."

interesting: boring.

kind: out of it; has lots of pets and a comb-over hairstyle.

lots of fun: alcoholic.

masculine: knuckles drag on ground, could use a full body wax.

mature: wears tweed; points with his pipe.

OK-looking: looks like a Clearasil ad "Before" shot.

perky: never stops talking.

petite: close to the ground, gnomelike, a bonsai.

poetic: limp, snuffly, inarticulate; avoids eye contact; wears black clothes that haven't been washed since the Carter administration.

politically active: likely to sprout rhetoric at any and all hours; talks in bumper-stickerspeak.

pretty: another double-standard word. For women: cute; for men: gay.

sensitive: a total wuss, highly strung.

settled/solid: has several children, station wagon, second mortgage.

shy: lives with mother.

spirited: for horses: crazy; for people: crazy.

spry: ancient, more wrinkles than a Shar-Pei puppy.

statuesque: mooselike, giant.

striking: facial features in an unorthodox arrangement.

the strong, silent type: thick as a brick, as sensitive as kielbasa.

stunning: has long, lustrous hair and flicks it around every ten seconds to make sure everybody knows it.

sweet: not too bright, smiles and nods a lot, emotionally about nine years old.

unique: bizarre.

unusual: just released/escaped from a padded cell; on parole.

vivacious: all over everyone like a cheap suit, like white on rice.

young at heart: old at waistline.

well-built/zaftig: top-heavy, preceded by her breasts by several minutes.

well-heeled/well off: but his morals have filed a Chapter 11.

Sex Guide for Puritans

1. Begin small talk about appreciation of beauty, importance of senses, physical endowments, etc.

2. Locate secondary sexual characteristics of spouse, if any.

3. Fondle briefly.

4. Go to bedroom. Together.

5. Turn out lights.

6. Locate spouse's naughty parts *down there*.

7. Fondle briefly.

8. Remove as few pieces of clothing around naughty parts as possible.

9. Place naughty parts close together. *Very* close together.

10. Bump together with spouse until you feel something nasty.

11. Take a long, hot shower and spray self with Lysol.

12. Pray for forgiveness.

13. Pretend nothing happened.

Recipe for First Love

2 fresh Hearts
1 qt. Love
2 cups Wine
½ cup Mixed Hormones
¼ cup Angst, Teenage
1 tbs. Passion*
1 tbs. Attraction
1 tsp. Affection
1 tsp. Vinegar or Lemon Juice
1 pinch each of Loneliness, Frustration, Honesty

Prepare hearts in advance by marinating separately in lukewarm emotions at room temperature. Sprinkle periodically with loneliness and frustration. After 12 years or so add hormones and raise heat. Stew for a few months, adding pinches of angst every other day. Lower heat and place hearts in one pan; simmer together. Stir in attraction, wine, and bring to full boil. Add passion. When soft, remove from heat, add three-quarters of love and whip hearts to a thick, syrupy sauce. Add affection, vinegar, and remainder of love. Coddle. Pour into cup until overflowing. Sprinkle with honesty to taste.   *Serves two.*

*Lust may be substituted for Passion if required

7

2: Translating the Personals

*Don't think that every sad-eyed woman has loved
and lost—she may have
got him.*

—Anonymous

What they say	What they mean
Man who knows what he wants requires woman who can give it.	Absolute jerk seeks mate with self-esteem low enough to put up with him.
Strong woman seeks appreciative man.	Pushy bitch seeks wimp with history of mother problems to boss around and humiliate.
Sensuous, clever, successful man needs suitable partner to share life's experiences.	Egocentric megalomaniac wants disciple to worship, cook, and clean up behind him.

Pretty, petite woman seeks mature, comfortable companion.

Gold digger would like to hear from elderly rich man with mansion, Rolls-Royce, and weak heart.

Me: handsome Tarzan. You: beautiful Jane. Let's meet and swing through the trees together.

Hunk with testosterone poisoning wants admirers he can take to parties and ignore while he leaves with someone else.

Model-type gal seeks equally put-together guy to make the best-looking couple ever.

Beautiful but shallow woman seeks equally beautiful and shallow man for totally meaningless relationship.

Traditional male seeks traditional female for traditional relationship.

Man totally out of touch with his feelings requires emotive female in order to feel complete.

Flapper type needs guidance from mature man.

Emotionally immature woman seeks daddy figure to tell her what to do and rescue her from actually acting her age.

Successful artist seeks established patroness.

Lazy bastard with artistic pretensions is looking for sucker to sponge off, preferably with own home and inherited wealth.

Quirky, attractive free spirit needs stable partner.

Mass of nerves with limited sense of own boundaries seeks focus for neurosis.

Experienced, busy man would like to find helpmate to share life's duties.

Overwhelmed single parent needs surrogate mother, live-in help, and cook all-in-one. No wages, occasional dinner out.

Appreciative older woman needs appreciative younger man.

Wife, bored with husband, seeks outside love interests on part-time basis.

Cary Grant type seeks Grace Kelly type for fun and friendship.

Man requires woman who cooks like mother, looks like princess, and makes love like professional.

Mature man wants to meet young, attractive consort for dinners, trips.

Middle-aged man, just escaped from twelve-year marriage, wants teenage girl to go with his new red convertible.

Intense, high-life loving woman needs dedicated, supportive mate/partner.

Addict is looking for rescuer to play do-gooder while she pretends to change her ways but doesn't.

Talented performer wants to meet woman with appreciation of the arts for cultural diversions.

Intelligent, avid scholar seeks man with similar interests.

Virile, family-oriented gentleman seeks receptive lady for fulfillment.

Mediocre musician seeks groupies.

Student would like to be married just long enough for spouse to put her through university.

Man looking to spawn as many children as possible with as many women as possible and never take responsibility for any of them.

The Post-date Postcard

*Saves decisions about whether to call
and who'll do it first.*

Thank you for the date, it was . . .

- ❑ wonderful.
- ❑ nice.
- ❑ better than staying home, I guess.
- ❑ about as much fun as a root canal without anesthesia.

The meal/film/play/show was . . .

- ❑ fascinating.
- ❑ interesting.
- ❑ all right, considering I didn't have to pay for it.
- ❑ stupefyingly boring, like you.

I thought you were . . .

- ❑ scintillating.
- ❑ sweet.
- ❑ better suited to someone else.
- ❑ an absolute, dyed-in-the-wool, card-carrying dweeb.

I would like to . . .

- ❑ see you again soon.
- ❑ see you again sometime.
- ❑ see you around, perhaps.
- ❑ see you in hell.

Truth in Advertising
At the Singles Bar

3: Directory of Opening Lines

Love doesn't make the world go 'round.
Love is what makes the ride worthwhile.

—Franklin P. Jones

Antique

I'm an etcher, you know—care to see my work? Shall we skip this dance and step out on the verandah? The moon is exceptionally beautiful tonight—would you care to accompany me on a little stroll?

Boy Scouts

Let's make fire

Crass

Are you married? Seeing someone? If so, is he/she bigger than me? Is she/he here? Do you have anything contagious? When you've finished that wanna come back to my place and fool around? I was wondering what you look like with your clothes off.

Esoteric

Don't you think Beethoven's treatment of Schiller's 'Ode to Joy' in the last part of the Ninth is a trifle heavy-handed? What's your feeling about Keynesian economics as it applies to unemployment in today's Pacific Rim? Don't you agree that Kant's work is undermined by its self-limiting solipsism? Have you ever considered the Reagan era as a Theater of the Absurd on the level of Beckett and Ionesco? Would you believe I have a complete set of the early Glenn Gould recordings at my apartment? How useful do you think it is to submit relatively small amounts of data to the Guttman-Lingoes Smallest Space Analysis? I think the problems of inner-city youth could be alleviated by reinstating rituals at puberty such as the Native American vision quest, don't you? How do you feel about Homer's choice of dactylic pentameter? Did you know the drink ring on your coaster looks like a Rorschach of a handcuff?

Gross

various slurping sounds, leering, whistles, primitive gestures.

Hearing Impaired

Who needs words?

Modern

Can I practice the Heimlich maneuver on you? How about some tiramisù and a double cappuccino? Is that a cellular phone in your pocket or are you just pleased to see me? I know a great place for a high colonic. I was thinking of buying a futon, too—can I check out yours? Wanna try some of my ginseng?

Morse

I'd like
to dot
your dash

Nautical

Let's get moored

Sex Guide for Car Mechanics

1. Cruise.
2. Align steering.
3. Adjust torque.
4. Loosen belts.
5. Check out bodywork.
6. Spread car cover.
7. Park car in garage.
8. Change oil.
9. Redline.
10. Recharge batteries.

4: Dating: The Grand Design

*If all the singles in the world were laid end to
end . . . it would save a hell of a lot of trouble.*
—D.W.

We've all seen the cartoon of caveman clubbing cave-woman over the head and dragging her back to his cave. This is, of course, a stupid and sexist view pandering to the basest of sophomoric taste, and bears no relation whatso-ever to actual historical fact.

In reality, cavemen dug *traps* for cavewomen to fall into. This was far less violent and didn't damage their skulls and hair as much. There was also the happy possibility of catching more than one.

At some point in the evolution of human culture, simply getting involved with your brother, sister, or close cousin must have been tried. The fact that there is now an almost universal taboo against incestuous relationships seems to indicate that the results of inbreeding were somewhat less than spectacular. Certain royal families today still show its unfortunate genetic repercussions.

In many early societies dating was rendered redundant, since a boy and a girl were often betrothed from birth. This was perhaps an attempt on the part of the parents to save their kids from the messy experimentation period of checking out the rest of the tribe. For the betrothed, though, it was a bit of a gamble. So these same societies also cleverly made divorce illegal, guaranteeing an enduring match whether or not the participants wanted it to be.

In those days you couldn't just jump in the car, drive to another town, and start over, after all. If you tried walking out on your assigned spouse, you were likely to be dragged back by the biggest dude in the village or pelted with large stones. Yes, once you were married you were married for good, and in some cases if your husband died before you, you'd be bumped off as well. To keep him company, presumably. Clean up after him in heaven, too, perhaps.

Indeed, all through human history societies have tried the betrothal method. Only comparatively recently, and only in the West, have couples been truly free to choose each other. Certainly mothers still want their daughters to marry doctors, and fathers still hate every boy their daughter brings home, but let's face it, these days nobody really listens to their parents.

This process of choice is acted out by *dating*. Dating is the system whereby two humans can check each other for mental imbalances, physical abnormalities, phobias, perversions, and financial instabilities. Today, this means that by going out together to eat overpriced undersized meals in overrated underlit restaurants, and imbibe mind-numbing quantities of alcoholic beverages, we are supposedly able to assess each other for compatibility of interest, intellect, sense of humor, and aura. Or at least achieve a state in which none of this matters.

This preliminary scrutiny is usually enough to cover a temporary liaison, long enough to explore each other's nether regions, and enough to discover whether or not the other person is worth staying with, worth opening up to, worth committing large chunks of one's life and income to, worth introducing to Mother, worth moving in with, getting a mortgage with, having offspring by, getting divorced from.

Dating is not infallible, though. Despite the most careful examinations most people are on their best behavior at first, only relapsing to their normal subhuman level once they know they've fully hooked another sucker. This is why so many relationships run aground a couple of years along. The dating examination was not performed fully, and all at once you wake up to find yourself next to some strange beast of indeterminate species. A creature that lives in its own world, doesn't wash its own plates, speaks in what might as well be monosyllabic Latvian curses, and who racks up phone bills worthy of a politician running for office. Someone who likes either the most juvenile of sitcoms or the most pompous and highbrow PBS programs, who either eats too much, not at all, or eats but defoods afterward; who, in short, suddenly stands naked before you in all his or her awful, flawed glory.

Thus dating is a crucial first stage, and it must be entered into with care and circumspection. Promises should not be prematurely made, commitments must not be committed to incontinently, seed should not be sown, or allowed to take root, indiscriminately.

Contrary to current belief, the ability to access five hundred satellite TV channels and almost every movie ever made has not replaced dating. Somehow, watching other people do something never quite seems to replace actually doing it oneself. No, dating is shrewdly designed to separate the wheat from the chaff, the men from the boys, the sane from the psychos. And short of telepathy, it's the best system we have.

Alternatives to Dating

Need a reason for not going back out into the wonderful world of singledom?

Watch reruns of anything, especially "The Love Boat."

Enter a monastery/nunnery and take vows of celibacy.

Build little shrines to a lost love.

Take up needlepoint, macramé, solitaire.

Join NASA and get sent to Mars.

Pretend you don't care.

Commit a felony and get imprisoned.

Contract a disfiguring disease of the skin.

Stay indoors and eat enormous quantities of high-cholesterol, high-sugar foods until you can no longer get through the door.

Dispense with personal cleanliness until you become a sort of roach motel.

Channel the spirits of seventeenth-century samurai warriors.

Dial vast amounts of 976 numbers.

Propose to your landlord/landlady.

What he imagined . . .

What he found . . .

What he settled for

5: What's Your Sign? Dates with Destiny

*The fault, dear Brutus, is not in our
stars, but in ourselves.*

—William Shakespeare, *Julius Caesar*

Aries need to prove they can conquer love.

ARIES
March 21—April 19

There's a reason this sign is represented by a ram. Head down, battering their way to the top, that's the Aries method. Love to them is like everything else—there to be mastered. They're enthusiastic and optimistic, sincere and idealistic, adventurous and individualistic, and a real pain in the ass. To the arrogant Aries everyone else is a little stupid and needs their leadership. Lovers can take a number and wait. Yet they don't like adoration—you have to be on their level or stay way behind. Your best bet with an Aries is to be cool and force them to conquer you, too.

Compatible signs are Leo and Sagittarius, and lots o' luck.

Taureans want to build a lasting love.

TAURUS
April 20—May 20

Like the bull, Taureans are slow, stolid, and earthy. Notoriously stubborn, they're resistant to change and fond of their domestic comforts. Their desires are simple and sensuous, and they have a tendency to get lazy and overdo the eating and drinking bit. For the most part they're patient and easy to deal with, but when they do eventually lose their cool all hell breaks loose. Taureans are not much use if you're looking for frivolous excitement and scintillating banter, but great if you want security tempered with a little romance.

Compatible signs are Capricorn, Virgo, and especially Scorpio. Bring food.

Geminis like the idea of love,
but they don't have much of an attention span.

GEMINI
May 21–June 21

Tired of just one lover? Try a Gemini—the closest you can get to legal bigamy. Two, yes *two* great personalities in one. Double the fun. Schizo without the phrenia. Fickle, unfocused, and inconsistent, yes, but quick-witted, charming, and fascinating, too. A Gemini can sell anyone on doing anything, then can be two hours late for it. As a mate they're a ticket to a roller coaster. They'll change their minds daily—

hourly—and if you don't like it they'll change you as well. For someone else.

Compatible signs are Libra, Aquarius, and especially Sagittarius. Hold on tight, now.

Cancers want love, and will be damned if anyone's going to steal it from them.

CANCER
June 22—July 21

Easygoing on the surface but game-playing and moody underneath, Cancerians can be just as crabby as their symbol. And like a crab they tend to grab hold and not let go, especially when it comes to money. They're secretive and reluctant to trust even those close to them, but eventually they'll open up. And inside they're sensitive, sympathetic, and sentimental. Since they're attracted to the finer things in life and like to save old things, perhaps they'll add you to their collection.

Compatible signs are Scorpio, Pisces, and especially Capricorn. Be inscrutable, and don't pry.

Love is OK with Leos as long as they're on top.

LEO
July 22–August 21

Leos are egos, extra-large and with added pompousness. Mini-tyrants that like to command, dominate, and for some reason always give advice. They see themselves as the kings and queens of life, and consequently they need the admiration of subjects. Like royalty, they can be overdramatic and overdressed, but they can carry it off. On the good side, they are open-hearted, faithful, generous, and throw damn good parties. Loving a Leo is fine if you're in the mood to be forever second in command.

Compatible signs are Aries, Sagittarius, and especially Aquarius. Be prepared to serve.

Virgos dissect love to see what makes it tick.

VIRGO
August 22—September 22

We're not really talking virgins here, but with the effort it takes to get close to a Virgo we might as well be. Low-key, twitchy, and around one or two on the charm scale, it can be difficult to enter their fastidious and hypercritical world. But these are practical, honest, and hardworking people, and they never look their age, so if they favor you with your loyal dedication you'll be lucky.

Compatible signs are Taurus, Capricorn, and especially Pisces. Hope you don't have any skeletons in the closet.

For Libras, love is a question
of weighing needs and wants.

LIBRA
September 23–October 22

Why the scales? Because Libras are forever debating the pros and cons. And they're half and half themselves— sweet and calm for a while, then cranky and argumentative. Intensely involved with work, then just as intensely sloth-like. They're sharp, artistic, and socially successful, but they're also selfish and won't win any medals for sensitivity. They like beauty, harmony, and truth and surround them-selves with exquisite things. So if your place is tidy and you're prepared to wait while they make up their mind, you stand a chance.

Compatible signs are Aries, Aquarius, and Gemini. Do the dishes.

To Scorpios, love is a fascinating trap.

SCORPIO
October 23–November 21

The heavy-duty sign. Watch where you tread with a scorpion around. Mysterious, hypnotic, and darkly intense, they're not to be trifled with. They'll never be pinned down, either, since they're too shrewdly secretive ever to really bare their souls. Besides, you're better off not knowing. Cool and composed on top but seething with passion underneath, this is the sign the others are afraid of. But Scorpio egos don't care, they even enjoy it. If you've been magnetized by one, you're in for an experience.

Compatible signs are Pisces, Cancer, and Aries for business. Armor is recommended.

Love is a game to Sagittarians,
and they're determined to win.

SAGITTARIUS
November 22–December 21

Is it possible to be painfully sharp and painfully blunt at the same time? It is if you're a Sagittarius. These are the Pollyannas of the Zodiac—idealistic, optimistic, overenthusiastic, and so likable it's amazing to witness. But not as amazing as their endless capacity for making tactless remarks. Luckily there's not an ounce of malice behind them. They just don't realize what they're saying, believing it's just honesty. So be prepared to be jabbed occasionally in the self-esteem by their accurate little arrows.

Compatible signs are Aries, Leo, and Gemini. Thicken your skin.

Love is acceptable to Capricorns
as long as it doesn't get out of hand.

CAPRICORN
December 22–January 20

Serious, cautious, and shy, Capricorns are sometimes hard to think of as lovers. They can seem unromantic, unsympathetic, and aloof. It's true that being involved with one can result in emotional malnutrition, but they can be devoted and even downright ardent at times. It's just that life is not a game to them. They're intensely ambitious and coolly determined to succeed. You'll also have to meet with the approval of their family, but at least you'll finally have someone worthy of taking home to yours.

Compatible signs are Taurus, Virgo, and especially Cancer. Dress warmly.

Love is the Aquarians' pie in the sky.

AQUARIUS
January 21–February 19

Sort of the eternal free-spirited hippie, Aquarians are spacy, absent-minded, and funny dressers. Not to mention always allergic to something. They're also inventive, unpredictable, psychic, and unquenchably curious about everyone. Loving freedom, they're hard to tie down to one relationship—they feel much more comfortable keeping things platonic. Your best bet is to realize that underneath their gregariousness they're lonely, and be unfathomable enough to make them take you on as part of their research.

Compatible signs are Gemini, Libra, and odd friendships with all other signs. Act weird.

Love is a supportive haven for Pisceans.

PISCES
February 20–March 20

Pisceans are supposed to be a mixture of all the other signs. They're unworldly, with little grasp of the everyday. They live outside in an emotional and temperamental objectivity that makes them elusive and unrealistic. This separateness can make them self-doubting and occasionally self-destructive, but it also makes them compassionate, wise, and whimsically imaginative. It's as if they know too much and sometimes need to compensate. Perhaps you can make them overindulge in you instead.

Compatible signs are Cancer, Scorpio, and especially Virgo.

Hell Dates

You know you're in for a bad dating experience when . . .

His '68 Pontiac station wagon is crammed to the roof with old newspapers.

She talks about wanting a child in the first three minutes.

He spends three hours talking about flagellation in the Middle Ages.

He has stigmata.

He starts to blow up long thin balloons at the restaurant table and twist them into animals.

Her eight children are waiting in her minivan.

His mother is in the backseat of the car.

He falls asleep over dessert.

She passes out *in* dessert.

He asks for the waitress's phone number.

Her breath melts the buttons on your coat.

His idea of a big night out is taking you for a large Slurpee and chili dog at the nearest 7-Eleven, then to a game of miniature golf, and you have to pay.

His kind of barbecue is going to a book burning.

She wants to know your bank balance before she'll even talk to you.

He has so much dandruff that when you open the door you think it's snowing outside.

She brings her teddy bear.

What she imagined . . .

What she found . . .

What she settled for

6: Let's Talk Relationshipese

Whoever named it necking was a poor judge of anatomy.
—Groucho Marx

Afraid of commitment
An accusatory phrase triggered anytime that the woman wants to do something the man doesn't.

Do you go out a lot?
Are you clean? Can I see your test results? Mind if we just stop by the clinic on our way back to your place and then wait six months or so?

Do you have a roommate?
Are there any obstacles between here and your bedroom?

I'd love to see where you live
a. I'd love to size up your standard of living.
b. OK—let's go for it.

I had a nice time, but . . .
. . . I made this pact with myself not to get involved with Martians.

I have a busy day/big day tomorrow
a. No, you can't come in.
b. No, I wouldn't have sex with you if it was my last night alive.
c. This whole evening was a serious mistake and if you don't mind I'm going to bed with chocolates and try to pretend it never happened and I hope you will, too.

I have a commitment
I wouldn't be seen with you if you were the last creature on earth.

I have an old friend visiting
The old boyfriend/girlfriend is back.

I have plans
a. But they don't include you.
b. Someone better-looking already asked me out.

I'm going with [name]
And when he/she finds out you asked me that, you're dead meat on a stick.

I'm in a relationship but it's not working out
So I'd be open to starting another with you if you like.

I'm involved with someone
And you're not worth getting uninvolved for.

I'm seeing someone, more or less
But I could more or less *not* see them anymore if you turn out to be more interesting.

I'm tied up for the next couple of days
Sorry—I seem to have appointments every night for the next ten years.

I'm very fond of you
a. I've always been fond of animals.
b. But you're just not my type.

I'm waiting for someone
Thank you, but I'd rather go home and clean the toilet than spend the evening with you.

I really care about you
a. But I've just fallen in love with someone else.
b. But I'm not physically attracted to you.
c. But I'm only sexually attracted to people I don't care about.

My lover and I are not getting along
My lover expects me to be *faithful*, for God's sake. Can you believe it?

We have an understanding
At least, as far as *I'm* concerned we have an understanding: I get to fool around.

We're just good friends
a. Not sleeping together;
b. No longer sleeping together;
c. Not sleeping together often;
d. Would be sleeping together if it weren't for the fact that one of us isn't interested.

You're just the kind of lover I'm looking for
You're just the opposite of the scumbag I've been seeing.

You seem like a nice person
a. What's wrong with you?
b. Sorry, but I was looking for someone who'll jerk me around.

Dating, 2001

1. Viewing of dating service videotapes.

2. Choice of video by code number.

3. Exchange of sexual history by modem.

4. Exchange of current photo by fax.

5. Credit check.

6. Police file check.

7. Health check.

8. Establishing of neutral territory.

9. Meeting in daylight with bodyguards.

10. Confirmatory exchange of voice mail messages.

11. Meeting without bodyguards.

12. Exchange of internet addresses.

13. Meeting in full protective bodysuits.

14. Mutual signing of pre-involvement contracts and insurance policies.

15. Experimental and noncommittal liaisons.

7: Rating the Love Gift

It is better to have old secondhand diamonds than none at all.

—Mark Twain

Anonymous gifts

1.2 Bad. The idea of gifts, at least as far as romance is concerned, is to get some mileage out of them. Giving anonymously may be noble, but noble schmoble when you run the risk of having your competition take the credit. Leaving the *price* on is tacky; leaving your name big and bold on box *and* inside—preferably engraved—is not.

Cards, sappy

1.7 Not the most romantic gift unless you know your lover's into schmaltz. Okay for anniversaries or a death in the family, not too effective at firing passion, except perhaps with nuns.

Cards, funny

2.0 Always good to be remembered with a smile. Handy for sending after you've said or done something totally inappropriate, as you probably tend to do. Not so good for deaths in the family.

Chocolates

2.9 Tricky, unless the object of your affection is a confirmed chocoholic. Otherwise they will no doubt think fondly of you for the three minutes it takes to eat them, but less so during the three weeks it takes to work off the extra pounds caused by the five thousand useless calories.

Pets

3.2 Not a good idea. Giving your loved one a small creature that will shed its hair all over the Persian rug, shred the silk designer upholstery, and defecate in assorted footwear is a questionable choice, no matter how cute. (Besides, they're only cute to begin with—it's nature's way of distracting parents from killing them.) Medium-sized animals like tigers, wolves, and cheetahs are still acceptable in arty circles, but eat vast amounts of messy raw meat. Large mammals like hippos and blue whales, while often touchingly affectionate, tend to be difficult to house and take for walkies.

Flowers

4.3 Good. Nearly always appreciated. One rose is a classy, understated token of affection; a dozen a splashy statement of the Big L. A roomful is still sometimes preferred by admirers of stage personalities but is generally considered just a little over the top. None of the foregoing applies to allergy sufferers, of course, with whom ragweed flowers are particularly unpopular. To be on the safe side, polite inquiries as to the state of your loved one's sinuses can save a budding relationship from withering in a fit of sneezing.

Music

5.1 Good for establishing romantic atmosphere, especially if it's slow, sexy stuff with sax and a soulful singer. Not so good if it's Sousa marches, *The 1812 Overture,* insect sounds of Madagascar, or any Fear album, though some people get turned on by the strangest sounds.

Show tickets

5.4 Perfect if you're the kind of person who doesn't have much to say. You've got at least two hours during which you can't converse even if you want to, and you have something to talk about afterward.

Sex toys

5.6 Well, why not? It'll either put the relationship on a whole new level or put you out on the street. One way or another it'll shake you both out of your rut. Just don't forget the batteries and/or keys.

A donation to a needy cause in your loved one's name

5.7 Okay, but more of a business than an intimate gift. Though a worthy sentiment, a charity receipt is not the most heart-fluttering proof of love. An engraved name on a museum wall is not too bad—at least someone can take friends to see it—but it's not exactly something to unwrap excitedly on Christmas morning.

Airline tickets

5.9 Very good, though they assume a certain intimacy. After all, going away somewhere presupposes staying together at the other end, so the first date or two may be a little premature. Otherwise a perfect gift, providing it's two *two*-way tickets to somewhere romantic, not one *one*-way to an underdeveloped Third World country currently at war or experiencing a cholera epidemic.

Mink coats

6.0 Formerly a 9, definitely a no-no these days. Unless your intent is that your inamorata gets spat on everywhere she goes, that is. Otherwise, clothing made from the *fur* of dead animals is out. Clothing made from *leather*, the *skin* of dead animals is still okay, but probably not for much longer. The leather rationale, presumably, is that the rest is already a Big Mac, so who cares? In general, avoid anything that had a face, unless it's a restaurant meal.

Billboards/Blimps/Skywriters

6.3 Impressive, extravagant, but ephemeral. For this gift to work its full magic it's very important to make sure your intended is around to witness the display, not off for a weekend in Vegas or in bed with the flu.

Rings/Jewelry

7.4 Classic. Guaranteed popularity. Doesn't matter if it's the wrong size, wrong shape, wrong stone color, or too ostentatious. It can always be exchanged, sold, melted down, or pawned. (Though diamonds, of course, are forever.) Just as long as it's real gold and some high-quality gemstones. Cubic Zirconia, no matter how huge, are a little tacky and won't get you laid.

Cosmetic surgery

8.0 Very touchy. This is a potentially volatile subject, unless you've been married for eons and you know your spouse wants to off a few chins or dispose of the jodhpurs. Otherwise you're just drawing attention to something that already makes them climb the walls, and *you'll* be the fat they cut from their life.

Expensive cars

9.7 One of the perennially favorite gifts, just as long as the pink slip is made out to the recipient and the loan to the giver. There's nothing quite like the subtle impact of a Porsche, BMW, or Mercedes in the driveway with a personalized license plate and a great big pink ribbon tied around it. Aston Martins, Jaguars, and Rolls-Royces are acceptable, too, and those sexy Italian Ferraris, Maseratis, and Lamborghinis are not usually frowned upon, either.

Mansions

9.8 Timelessly appropriate. For the truly successful, nothing says "I love you" more than a little 15-bedroom, 10-bath shack on 4 wooded acres with pool, tennis court, and servants' quarters. Other gifts pale beside property, since owning a piece of the planet is promising someone the world and really delivering.

Tropical Islands

10.9 For those fortunate few whose affections and affluence are boundless, a small South Pacific atoll with crystal-clear lagoon and pristine white sands dotted with coconut palms makes the ideal anniversary present. With its complement of yacht, dune buggy, and an unlimited supply of Dom Perignon on ice, this is the ultimate gift.

Sex Guide for Trekkies

1. Lay in course for desired celestial body.

2. Enter gravitational pull.

3. Maintain geosynchronous orbit.

4. Check suitability of atmosphere.

5. Beam down to surface.

6. Explore new world.

7. Raise shields.

8. Open shuttle bay doors.

9. Boldly go where no one has gone before.

10. Warp ten.

11. Fire photon torpedoes.

12. Leave orbit.

13. Return to Starbase.

The Racecar Driver's Love Letter

My darling teammate—
I was fresh out of the showroom when we met, so to speak. All the optional extras, still in cherry condition, cranked up for the open road and eager to get my pedal to the metal.

You and I spiritually sideswiped each other outside that bar, and from that moment on we paced the racetrack of our youth. Sleek, you were, and well-built. I was all power and noise, full of my own speed, always in overdrive.

We hit the open road in partnership, shiny and new. Burning rubber in search of some elusive destination—the road to riches, perhaps. For three wonderful years we drove each other farther, higher. Three years of top-down, flat-out, fast living. Until the day I made a wrong turn.

You were happy to go on joyriding, I know. It was me that put on the brakes. I said I thought we ought to throttle back, maybe get hitched. Well, I guess my timing was off. I should've known we couldn't run a high-octane relationship on cheap gas. And you can't keep a high-performance engine idling without fouling up the sparks.

I steered us wrong, I know now. Our new direction turned out to be a detour down a one-way street, with no U-turns. And we'd never had to deal with each other in a parked position before. Suddenly it seemed our feelings stalled and we couldn't jump-start them. We'd left behind every thing we had in common. On the road. On *our* road.

One day you backed out of my arms and hit the blacktop alone, taking my heart with you. I puttered around, running on empty, looking for someone else to recharge my battery. I drove around in circles, aimlessly cruising; my life hopelessly out of alignment, un-tuned. I was all over the map. I had missed my exit on the freeway of life. I was a wreck.

Then one day, while I was still stuck in the emotional slow lane, you passed by. Still fast, still in good shape. But I could still keep up with you, too—we were still well matched. I pulled alongside, and I've kept up ever since.

And now, side by side we drive love's highway.

Your ever-loving co-driver

47

II

Mating

8: Lovetalk: Sweet Somethings

Never go to bed mad. Stay up and fight.
—Phyllis Diller

Pet Names for Each Other

Traditional

Honey, Baby, Sweetheart, Dear, Lover, Darling, Sugar, Pumpkin, Angel, Precious, Beautiful, My Better Half, Pickle, Pet, Sweetiepie, Kitten, Tiger, etc.

Poetic

Love of My Life, My Helen of Troy, Lambkin, My Lancelot, My Guinevere, Mon Amour, Mi Amore, My Leading Lady/Man, Girl/Man of My Dreams, My Inamorata, My Moment Supreme, Nearest to My Heart, Tropic Sunset, Apple of My Eye, etc.

Colloquial

Molasses Butt, Ratlegs, Snooky-Ookums, Love Handles, Stinky, Boogernose, Shithead, Sweetcheeks, Stupid, Thunderthighs, Love Puppy, Hey You, Whatsyour name, etc.

Pet Names for Each Other's Genitalia

Traditional

HIS: Manhood, Member, Organ of Procreation, Reproductive Organ, Family Jewels, It, Ohmigod, That Thing, and for some reason a lot of first names: Peter, Johnnie, Dick, Willie, Little Elvis, etc.

HERS: Thingummy, Pudendum, Womanhood, Waterworks, Down There, Plumbing, Privates, You Know Where, That Thing, etc.

Poetic

HIS: Priapus, Babymaker, Dart of Love, John Thomas, Membrum Virile, Jade Stem, Shaft of Cupid, etc.

HERS: Jade Gate, Gateway to Heaven, Venus's Glove, Altar of Hymen, Cave of Harmony, Flower of Chivalry, Garden of Eden, Lotus, Love's Pavilion, etc.

Colloquial

HIS: Baloney, Dipstick, Binkle, Gigglestick, Trouser Trout, Tootsie Roll, Mr. Happy, Pecker, Tube Steak, Wang, Weenie, Wish-Wand, etc.

HERS: Booty, Cookie, Honeypot, Muffie, etc.

Pet Names for Using Each Other's Genitalia

Traditional

Sexual Intercourse, Having Sex, Doing It, Making Love, Getting Intimate, Making Babies, Consummation, Going All the Way, Fun and Games, Fooling Around, Marital Duty, Rutting, Relations, Playing Mommies and Daddies, You Know What, etc.

Poetic

Making the Beast With Two Backs, Carnal Gymnastics, Amorous Congress, Connubial Bliss, Coitus, Act of Love, Conjugal Act, Swiving, etc.

Colloquial

Boinking, Boffing, Jumping the Bones, Bedpresses, Mattress Dancing, Flesh Session, Tumbling and Diving, Hide-the-Salami, Cars and Garages, Horizontal Jogging, Bouncy-Bouncy, Shtupping, Rolling in the Hay, Parking the Porpoise, The Ol' In and Out, Getting It On, Riding the Pink Pony, Nookie, etc.

Sex Guide for Seniors

Warning! The following may be hazardous to your health. Consult your doctor before attempting any of the actions listed.

1. Make sure your wills are in order.

2. Move close to check if you're with the right partner.

3. Lock walkers.

4. Mash dentures.

5. Get nurse to guide you to a bedroom.

6. Remember to ask nurse to leave.

7. Grasp whatever you can reach easily.

8. Remove as much clothing as you can without getting exhausted.

9. Place bodies together and hope they remember what to do.

10. Ring for nurse to resuscitate your partner.

9: Introducing the Lease-a-Lover™ Program

Everyone winds up kissing the wrong person goodnight.

—Andy Warhol

No more shopping around

The one-step love shop! *Lease-a-Lover*™ (formerly Harry's House O' Love) has all the lovers you could hope for—*and all conveniently under one roof!* Let your eyes do the walking and your glands do the talking! Choose the model you like, and on approval of your good credit* take him/her home! No dating, no waiting!

Save money, time

No more costly and tiring nights on the town while you try to find your dream lover! No more hanging around in sleazy bars breathing secondhand smoke! No more wasted months finding out whether that stranger is the stranger for you! Pick the right one from the start when you *lease* your lover!

---

*Small down payment required. Clothing, taxes, license, and optional equipment extra.

52

Big selection

All colors, from ebony to albino! All widths, from wiry to pleasantly plump! All heights, from midget to giant! All ages, from jailbait to dirty old man! And of course, all sexual preferences! Yes, if God made 'em, *Lease-a-Lover*™ stocks 'em!*

No muss, no fuss

We feature only healthy models fully checked out by our trained staff. Clean and relationship-ready, all of our lovers earn their own living, dress themselves, and behave politely with company. What they do in private is *up to you*!!!**

Take a test drive

Can't decide? Ask about our *One-Day Free Play*. Try out a lover for one day before you sign—and remember, that's *one night*, too!***

We want your trade-in

Bring us your old, your tired, your worn-out clunker! We'll be happy to give you Blue Book price on any used lover—*no matter what model year or condition!* Just bring 'em in and we'll deduct the price from a brand-new one!

Money-back guarantee

If any *Lease-a-Lover*™ lover performs below expectations, develops an embarrassing habit, contracts a disease, or dies on the job, just return for an exchange—no questions asked****. We're not satisfied unless *you're* satisfied! We have a suitor to suit you!

*Subject to stock on hand. Some models not available in all areas.
**Subject to all applicable city, state, and federal laws.
***No purchase necessary. Small refundable insurance deposit required.
****Damage due to mishandling, drugs, or bad food will be billed to lessee.

No messy endings

Our five year* lease gives you the perfect length relationship. You get a lover for as long as the feelings are fun, fresh, and mutual. Then—it's back to the showroom for a new one! No sordid scenes, no tears, no divorces, and *no attorneys!*

The relationship of the future—*now*

Yes, for the future you always wanted, the *Lease-a-Lover*™ program is the only way to go. It's the twenty-first century way of loving—speedy, simple, and safe. And best of all, *temporary*. It's all at your local *Lease-a-Lover*™ showroom today!**

Don't leave it up to Stupid Cupid, get *a new lease on love!*

*Optional extension to seven years if still in love.
**If you can't find a showroom, call our toll-free number for a free catalog.

Sex Guide for Film Directors

1. Establish scene.

2. Opening dialogue.

3. Assign grips.

4. Lock extreme close-up.

5. Dolly in.

6. Ensure coverage.

7. Deep focus.

8. Rapid montage.

9. Build to climax.

10. General release.

11. Lap dissolve.

12. Fade out.

10: Origin of Species II: The Sequel

It was not the apple on the tree, but the pair on the ground, I believe, that caused the trouble in the garden.

—M. D. O'Connor

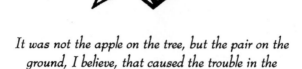

A new view of human differentiation, with apologies to Darwin.

Scientists have finally proved something the rest of us have suspected all along—that men and women are from different planets.

Yes, recent discoveries indicate that our two sexes are not originally of the same species but actually represent a case of parallel evolution. That is, we evolved similarly but separately. And during some enchanted eon of our mutual hominid past, we discovered each other.

Men, or perhaps we should now say *homo homo*, did in fact descend from apes here on Earth. *Homo gyna*, however, evolved on a planet much like this but revolving around a different, distant sun. Each environment apparently suited the development of bipedal creatures, and nature seems to have decided upon a similar physical structure.

Each species originally reproduced by parthenogenesis, an efficient, if rather boring, means of reproduction that requires no sex partner. Men sometimes had, we can speculate, particularly intense dreams about strange men with bald faces and bumps on their chests, and this triggered conception. Their children—all male, of course—were born somewhat painfully and brought up on fermented fruit juices, there being little in the way of father's milk.

Women, on the other hand, may well have had occasional, equally powerful fantasies about unusually hairy-faced women with additional appendages and became pregnant in this fashion. They were luckily a little better equipped to bring forth their girl children, and this is possibly why women don't seem to resent their progeny as much as men.

Being evolved from apes, men had a tendency to hang around in trees a lot, dropping their rinds and socks whenever they felt like it, forgetting where they left their children while in a fermented juice stupor, and generally making a bit of a mess of Africa. It's not hard to imagine roving bands of unkempt males beating their chests at one another, playing brutally competitive games in which the losers were maimed for life, and staying out till all hours. Beds would never have been made, toilet seats permanently left up, bristles left in every washbasin. Food would be eaten wherever it was found, and indeed plates have been unearthed that were apparently used for meals over and over again without ever being washed, being discarded only when they became too heavy to hold.

The women, on their planet, seem to have evolved from a minklike animal—esthetically proportioned, graceful, and vicious when cornered. We can hypothesize that they would spend their time grooming themselves and each other, and then sit around on Friday and Saturday nights, waiting. None of their gadgets would have worked for long, there being no one to fix them, and their fingernails would have been permanently broken from trying. Their lawns must have grown very tall and scruffy, while their homes probably stayed amazingly neat.

In order to look for a more fulfilling life, one in which they could be far less independent and preferably be paid less for doing twice as much work, women must have decided to look elsewhere. Perhaps they built a spaceship, or possibly they hitched a ride on some spacefaring aliens' interstellar bus, getting off at Earth.

At any rate, fossilized remains make it clear that women developed an enclave around their landing site, which was no doubt soon discovered and visited by curious homo homos. The men must have been pleasantly surprised by the unexpected appearance of these creatures of their dreams, just as the women must have been overjoyed at this materialization of the mysterious dark, handsome strangers they had imagined.

It was at this point that women apparently felt the need to civilize the indigenous inhabitants of Earth. Cheerfully, they set about rescuing men from their nasty savage natures. This must not have been a particularly successful endeavor, since to this day they're still trying to teach men to clean up after themselves and lay off the fermented juices, and still have to buy their clothes for them.

Men, for their part, resented being coerced out of their trees, and in reaction are still trying to take the women they meet upstairs. From the start they made a concerted effort to de-civilize the women and have succeeded in undoing much of the progress women had made before their fateful visit. It's from deep racial memories of this dynamic that women's feelings of being hampered by men originate, and men's feelings of being manipulated.

Fortunately the close proximity of the two types of being caused a muddling of sensory perceptions, a chemically triggered cessation of rational thought that we now call *love*. Love made it temporarily possible to ignore these incredibly daunting differences and caused the two species to attempt to interact. This created the misconception of love being all that is needed to get along with one another, a theory we now recognize as hopelessly naive.

Since neither species spoke the other's language— indeed it is doubtful if men *had* a language other than negative or positive grunts—new words had to be coined for them to be able to understand one another. The failure of this new language is only too evident today, when men and women, ostensibly using the same words, still don't have the faintest idea what the other is talking about.

Despite, or perhaps because of, this misunderstanding, men and women paired off, presumably to further explore interplanetary communication. Thus began dating, and since at first all women looked alike to all men (bald-faced, bumps on chest), and all men looked alike to women (hairy, extra appendages), they would exchange special markers, worn on the fingers. This was the invention of the wedding ring, still just as ineffective today as an indicator of who supposedly belongs to whom.

Nevertheless, a new tradition had been born that continues to the present, millions of mismatched years later. Few men still carry their own babies to term, choosing instead to interact on an interplanetary level with the alien species. Some of the differences men have noticed have come in handy for feeding the offspring of their cosmic union, though babies would have been a lot quieter when fed solely on fermented juice. And women have found that some of the men's differences are useful for passing Friday and Saturday nights.

But differences there are, and at last they are illuminated in the light of these new discoveries. No longer need we struggle to understand why the sexes have such trouble getting along. With relief we can finally acknowledge that we are not two sexes of a single species, but *two species* enduring a fragile and unnatural symbiosis.

It should be no surprise, then, that there often seems to be such a gulf between men and women. Being single is our natural state; divorce simply a return to our original, innate condition. Therefore let us not take it too personally when relationships founder. It's an achievement that they exist at all. It's a tribute to the stubbornness of human nature that we've even come this far, and we should be proud.

Perhaps, if we continue to try, in another million or so years women and men may eventually come to some kind of amicable understanding.

And who knows, it may even be worth it.

Love Etiquette

It's not considered cool to:

Commit adultery on your honeymoon.

Leave little curly hairs on the soap.

Start reading during intimacy.

Fall asleep during foreplay.

Chew gum while kissing, unless you're exchanging it.

Seduce your children's lovers.

Seduce your parents' lovers.

Publish ratings of your sexual partners in the local newspaper.

Pimp for your lover.

The Programmer's Love Letter

My little WYSIWYG—

You and I had been peripherals in each other's lives for some time, then, after being set up by friends, we belatedly realized we were compatible. We shared the same system, the same number of bytes. Soon we interacted, and bit by bit we interfaced.

I was attracted to your display resolution, your text arrays, your spline curves, your drive. I dreamed of your modeling matrices, your fill style, the flexibility of your shading algorithms. I found myself plotting to multitask together, bringing over batches to process each evening.

You seemed to like my intensity profile, my key-in commands, my primitive attributes. You appreciated my input, respected the quality of my hardware, the number of my chips. You learned to love my logic.

And so we time-shared, hardwired our subroutines, exchanged software. We spent more and more of our realtime learning each other's language, searching memories, exploring each other's archival subsystems.

I took you to my mainframe and set up a workstation for you. You allowed me random access to your core. We shared a database; went online. We crunched numbers on spreadsheets, nesting.

Late at night we could always be found deeply immersed in testing our Boolean formulas, stretching our eigenfunctions. We did everything together: matrix manipulation, associative dimensioning, Phong shading. Not to mention comparing our non-uniform rational surfaces.

I don't know what happened then. Perhaps we didn't allow enough intervals in our routine, didn't include failsafe diagnostics in our run-time. Maybe we started to experience signal drift and noise interfered with our program, maybe we had bad sectors, a TIFF. Whatever it was, one day our linkage ceased; our relationship became terminal. You dumped me, I offloaded you.

And yet, though I know we will never compute together again, you will always be coded deep within my circuitry.

Forever, Floppy:)

11: Types of Sex

Lord give me chastity—but not yet.
—Saint Augustine

Atheistic
Oh, oh, oh, oh, oh, oh, *nobody!*

Bestial
Honey? Have you seen Spot? Irving, I don't think that's what's meant by *animal husbandry*.

Bisexual
Effectively doubles the dating choice. Handy for small towns.

Bizarre
No honestly, Shirley, I quite like hanging upside down—it's just that all the blood rushes to by doze.

Hurry up and finish sniffing my shoes, Frank, I have to wear them tonight.

More Cool Whip, cupcake?

Creative/experimental
Let's see . . . last night was the hammock. Tuesday was the Checker cab, Monday the Elks Club roof, and Sunday the church lawn. How about either the appliance

department at Sears or the announcer's box at the hockey game?

Fantasy/masturbation

The safest sex. Besides, you get a better class of lover.

Group

Whose *is* this?

Indifferent/lazy

I suppose so . . . (yawn) . . . Climb on, then. Don't take too long, though.

Insensitive

Oh, guess I'd better go now, Mom—Ted's losing his erection, and you know how scarce they are these days.

Manipulative

Let's do a sixty-eight—you do me and I'll owe you one.

OK/nice

Well, that was . . . nice. Was it nice for you? Jolly good. Gosh, is that the time? Must be going. Thanks again. It's been, uh, nice.

Promiscuous

Mmmmmm—love you too, Jack. 'Bye. *Next!*

Role-Playing

I thought Napoleon put his hand in *his* shirt.

Martha, if you're doing Salome again tonight, can we at least close the curtains first?

No, Ralph, not the Norman Bates—I was gonna take a shower.

Sado-Masochistic/B&D

I have some lovely new sheepskin restraints for tonight, dearest.

I thought you were going to polish the leather teddy today.

We seem to be out of salt for your wounds, hon—will sand be OK?

Torrid/passionate

Oh baby oh baby oh baby oh oh oh oh. *Oh*. Pass me the fire extinguisher, would you?

Sex Guide for Computer Programmers

1. Assess compatibility.

2. Interface on primary levels.

3. Exchange software.

4. Explore each other's subsystems.

5. Employ surge protector.

6. Activate hard drive.

7. Access core.

8. Run program.

9. Download.

10. Exit.

2: Bad Things to Say During Lovemaking

Romance, like alcohol, should be enjoyed but must not be allowed to become necessary.

—Edgar Z. Friedenberg

For a woman

Ick. Is that all there is? That reminds me—I forgot to get wieners. Don't you just *hate* these cottage cheese ceilings? Is that a burglar downstairs? Do you think that the pasta was *al dente* enough? I heard the market was soft today, too. That's OK—it happens to everyone sometimes. It's not the size that counts. Ugh, that's *disgusting*. Don't mess up my lipstick. Is that the time already? D'you think I should wear the pearls tomorrow night? I had a lover once who could do it twelve times a night. That Bill sure is a hunk.

For a man

What d'you call these? Hmmm, better lay off the desserts, babe. Let's get this over with before the game. Move your head to one side so I can see the screen. Ooooh, Mommy. Ooooh, Louise . . . I mean Donna. Sorry—*Jackie*, that's it, isn't it? What about them Dodgers? What's a clitoris? OK, I'm done—what's in the refrigerator? Was it good for you? Zzzzzzzz.

For a parent

How're you two doing in there? I just made some hot chocolate—I'll bring you in some. How about some cookies? Did the light bulb burn out again? I've got another here I can replace it with. Is my TV Guide in there? I'll bring Granddad in and we can all watch reruns of "Little House on the Prairie."

For a roommate

Phone call for you, Marcie! Got any postage stamps? Can I borrow your black leotard? Hey, which one's in there with you this time? Where's the remote? Where's the cat? You know that guy you're seeing?—I saw him with someone else at lunch today.

For a child

Mommy! Daddy! *Mommy! Daddy!* I think the kitchen's on fire. There's some men in uniforms at the door. I'm gonna watch this *Nasty Nurses* tape, OK? I'm hungry and I'm gonna eat all the candy in the house. I can't turn the bathroom taps off. What's that noise in there? Are you hurting each other? Jeremy's drinking the stuff under the sink. I think my gerbil is in your bed.

The Post-problem Postcard

Spackle over those spats with this easy multiple choice mailer:

Dear . . .

❑ Sweetheart
❑ Lover
❑ Sir/Madam

I'm truly sorry we . . .

❑ had that misunderstanding.
❑ had that brawl.
❑ had that kid.

I feel . . .

❑ like a fool.
❑ like a heel.
❑ like a beer.

I'm truly sorry I . . .

❑ said those things.
❑ did those things.
❑ ever met you in the first place.

We really must . . .

❑ get together and patch things up.
❑ get married.
❑ get attorneys.

Please . . .

❑ say you'll forgive me.
❑ say you'll come back.
❑ return my underwear.

13: Debunking Sexual Mythology

Q: What is premature ejaculation?
A: There's no such thing. Some of us are simply
very busy men.

—Tym Manley, *Punch*

A man's ideal woman is a nymphomaniac living over a liquor store.

Untrue. Living with a nymphomaniac would just increase a man's performance anxiety to its maximum, and since large quantities of alcohol inhibit sexual performance this fantasy could never become an effective reality.

A stiff dick knows no conscience.

Partially true. When a man gets aroused all the blood temporarily leaves the conscience area of his brain to fill certain other regions.

Caucasians lack virility.

This is, of course, reverse racism of the worst kind. Just because they have no natural rhythm and can't dance obviously has no carryover effects in the bedroom, otherwise *they* would be a minority.

Men are insensitive to women's needs.

Needs? What needs?

Men aren't interested in foreplay.

Men most definitely *are* interested in this appetizer, as it were, to the erotic entrée. The misunderstanding stems from a difference between the sexes in their interpretation of the word *foreplay*. Women tend to think of it as a physical expression of affection and a sensual exploration lasting anywhere from twenty minutes to four hours. Men, on the other hand, tend to think of it as a couple of quick drinks then a frenzied grappling with buttons, hooks, and zippers sometimes lasting as long as three minutes.

It *is* true, on the other hand, that men are generally not interested in *after*play, or post-orgasmic touching. For most males this is Miller time, a chance for a smoke, or to see what's on the zzzzz channel.

Men have to have an orgasm once they're aroused.

This is a fiction perpetuated by teenage boys who want to get beyond first base to fourth or fifth. They make it sound as if the repercussions of stopping petting before complete carnal consummation will be extreme pain, turning colors in the blue palette, and some kind of major, inoperable hernia. In actual fact the adolescent male very early gets used to the frustration of rampant but unalleviated hormones and is quite adept at either steaming quietly or employing Mr. Wrist. Very few have been known to detonate.

Men often climax too soon/Women often take too long.

It's true that some women seem to order their orgasm from out of state, mailed third class with insufficient postage. It's also true that some men tend to achieve theirs so quickly that if you blink he's already back at the swimsuit issue of *Sports Illustrated*. Luckily, though, there is not yet a federally mandated OSHA standard for Length of Elapsed Time Before Orgasm. Somewhere between three seconds and three hours seems to be the national norm, with one minute being the male average; thirty for women. Coming together regularly is considered a rare enough occurrence to warrant the awarding of the Distinguished Service Order by the Vice President, or, in the United Kingdom, a telegram from the Queen.

The only true, mature orgasm for a woman is a vaginal orgasm.
This fallacy stems from old misunderstandings of the nature and function of the clitoris. Besides, as most women will tell you, any orgasm is a good orgasm, no matter what its source. Zelda M of Dallas, for instance, is quite happy with overwhelming feelings emanating from her left big toe.

Women are too emotional.
Emotional? EMOTIONAL? WHADDAYOU MEAN *EMOTIONAL?*

Women don't know what they want.
Nonsense. Every woman wants something different, that's all, whereas men all want the same thing.

The Multiple Choice Love Letter

My . . .

❑ own true love

❑ old buddy

❑ distant acquaintance

I . . .

❑ think about you every waking minute.

❑ think about you sporadically.

❑ think about you, then I take a Tylenol.

You . . .

❑ mean everything to me.

❑ mean more to me than most I've slept with.

❑ mean I've made another horrible mistake.

We . . .

❑ feel so right together.

❑ feel so wrong together.

❑ feel like warm Jell-O together.

Can we . . .

❑ meet at the altar soon?

❑ meet at the motel soon?

❑ try and forget we ever met?

Won't you . . .

❑ be my one and only true love?

❑ be my occasional pop-tart?

❑ be my janitor?

Sex Guide for the CIA

1. Reconnoiter areas of involvement.

2. Undermine and destabilize defenses.

3. Veto policy of nonintervention.

4. Explore infrastructure of private sectors.

5. Initiate debriefing.

6. Utilize protective devices.

7. Target bases.

8. Deploy ordnance.

9. Escalate undercover operations.

10. Detonate payload.

11. R & R.

14: Lovesick: Illnesses of the Heart

Love, the itch, and a cough cannot be hid.
—Thomas Fuller, M.D.

Baldness

Recent studies indicate that Male Pattern Baldness (MPB), previously thought to be genetically inherited, is actually caused by relationship stress. Triggers are thought to be running fingers repeatedly through the hair in exasperation, scratching the scalp in puzzlement, and intense cranial activity due to anxiety. Tests on a control group of men who were locked in a room for five years with only an inflatable doll for company show no significant hair loss. (Some conversational skills, however, were impaired.) Another group of men, of similar ages and backgrounds but with live mates, showed major amounts of MPB. These findings appear to suggest that to keep your hair—lose your lover. Or vice versa.

Cellulite

Yes, it's a little-known fact that unhappy affairs generate cellulite. The act of falling in love causes fat cells in the thigh to expand from the excitement, which help give that familiar glow displayed by those newly in love. The downside of this effect, however, is the collapse of those fat cells as soon as the fling has flung. Those with cellulite can thus wear it proudly as a sign of experience, a dimpled memento to loves lost. And, by extension, too many bad relationships may eventually lead to liposuction.

Jealousy
The green-eyed monster is bred by the need to possess a loved one entirely, combined with a shaky self-image, so that any time the sufferer is away from the love object fantasies of betrayal occur. This is often a self-fulfilling prophecy, since even if they weren't betrayed to begin with, jealous lovers start to act so badly that they effectively push their partners into the arms of someone else.

Lost Friends
Falling *in* love often equals falling *out* with chums. Sudden change from best buddy to someone who cancels dates and no longer returns calls is bound to lose all but the most devoted, or masochistic, of friends. If the happy couple stay happy, they shouldn't alienate anyone who might later be a good source of engagement, wedding, and baby shower gifts. If they split, they'll need all the support they can get.

Loss of Appetite
An often forgotten but always effective diet plan is to fall head over heels in love with someone, preferably someone indifferent to your affections. This causes a mixture of excitement and anxiety that fills the stomach, formerly called "pining away." It is, however, a strictly temporary solution to losing weight. Its ideal conclusion is the happy blossoming of a new relationship with the object of your devotion. Then, food will be several steps down your priority list, at least for a while. Rejection, on the other hand, usually undermines the slimming effects and causes a return to eating as a comfort and consolation.

Lost Mind

Though love doesn't cause as much madness lately as it seemed to in Victorian times, the phenomenon is still sometimes encountered today. A century ago, when a woman would swoon given half a chance—possibly because she was crammed into a whalebone corset—an unhappy love affair was considered a good excuse for locking oneself into a hut on a windswept English moor and howling "Heathcliff!" at the full moon for the rest of your days. Nowadays, luckily, we have shrinks and Prozac for that kind of thing. Nevertheless, the crazed cuckold, the wacked-out widow, the lover left for another still sometimes flip out dramatically enough to damage themselves and/or others. They should be treated with compassionate understanding for the first month or so, then, if the condition persists, given a good slap.

Social, and Not-So-Social, Diseases

Sometimes a little more than happiness gets spread around. Not a subject to be made light of, a little care and preparation can save a lifetime of misery. A *short* lifetime of misery.

Stand By Your Man Syndrome

Comes from listening to too many Country & Western lyrics. So what if he's convicted of murdering all of his former girlfriends and burying them beneath his mobile home? He's changed, he's mine, and I love him.

Places to Find Potential Romance

Good	Bad
The microwave-meals-for-one section of the supermarket.	Death Row at a maximum-security prison.
The weekly meeting of the "Single and Desperate" Club.	At the crack dealer's. Divorce Court.
Christmas parties of Fortune 500 companies.	Monasteries and nunneries.
Safe deposit departments of Swiss banks.	Waiting at the surgeon's for a sex change operation.
Jewelers in Beverly Hills.	Early-warning radar stations above the Arctic Circle.
Rolls-Royce repair shops.	Turkish prison cells.
Laundromats in Monaco.	The terminal ward.
	Lamaze classes.
	Meetings of Murderers Anonymous.

The Love Measure

How do I love thee?
Let me count the ways.

—Elizabeth Barrett Browning

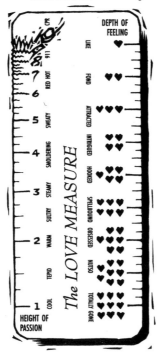

15: The Stages of Love

The course of true love never did run smooth.
—William Shakespeare, *A Midsummer Night's Dream*

From Tender Loving Care to Temporary Restraining Order. Or, the past tense of smitten is smut.

1. Indifference

Not bad, but I'll be damned if I'll phone her first. I'll do him a favor and see him one more time. Oh, I suppose so, I was only going to exfoliate tonight. Why not?—there's no sports on TV, and I can trim the hairs in my nostrils anytime. All right, but just don't expect anything, OK?

2. Gaga/smitten/batshit

This is the real McCoy. Wow. Hot damn. Finally, Mr./Ms. Right! I think about her every waking second. I wonder what she's doing now—is she thinking about me? I'll just wait by the phone for three weeks for his call. Flowers! How sweet! I want to tell the whole world. Where has he been all my life? This is it—marriage, babies, the works. She's the love of my life. Everyone else was just training for this. I was never really, *really* in love before. I could talk to him all night. I'll see him in my dreams. I could make love with her for eternity. I don't care about my AT&T bill. I love his moles. She's better than Monday night football. I'd rather see her than go with the gang to a game. He's better than calories derived from fat. I'm having her name tattooed across something or other!

3. Rose-tinted glasses/The fantasy
He's perfect. She's just what I was always looking for—smart, good-looking. What cheekbones, what eyes, what abs, what pecs. We're the quintessential lovers—no one else ever loved the way we do. Amazing how fate conspired to make our paths cross. Just think—if I hadn't trodden on her poodle while jogging in the park that day we might never have met. We look so good together. Eat your hearts out, girls. Wait till the guys get a load of this.

4. Mushbrain
Oh, schnookiepoo. Oh, picklepecker. Oh, sweetiecakes. Oh, bottyboos. Oh, snugglepuppy. Oh, binklebumper.

5. Coming down to earth/The honeymoon is over
Are those his socks again? He sweats—I never noticed. She had a *zit* this morning, for God's sake. He drools when he's asleep. What, it's against the law if I just want to go to bed and *sleep* for once? Are you really wearing that *again?* Sure, I'm going out with the boys—so what?

6. Irritating mannerisms/Falling off the pedestal
If you scratch your butt before coming to bed *one more time*, buddy, you can sleep in the garage. When I said "Don't ever change," I wasn't referring to your underwear. Hey, if you're going to spend so much time in the bathroom, I think we should put a couch and magazines out here in the hall.

7. Hard cold reality/Who is this person?
What on earth was I thinking of? What *is* this creature I've been shacking up with? This isn't the wonderful person I fell in love with—this is *Australopithecus*. Have I been in

a coma for the last two years? Do I have cataracts? This is just a bad dream, right? I think I just woke up in the wrong life.

8. Nothing in common

This was a biggggg mistake. How do I get out of this? Perhaps he'll just die. Maybe she'll be transferred . . . to Antarctica. I just won't go home, ever again. Where can I get a fake ID? What if I just closed out my account and caught the next flight to Paris? What if I just pretend to have amnesia and can't remember ever meeting him?

9. New understandings

Okay, I'll mow the lawn if you do the dishes. All right, I won't criticize your lovemaking if you don't keep talking all the time. I know it's true that whenever you try to get intimate I hide in the closet, but I'm working on it.

10. Boredom

Oh? You were away for the weekend?—I didn't notice. Would you mind sleeping in another room in the future, uh, what was your name again? Donald, are you asleep with your eyes open? I've got a great idea—let's pretend we still care about each other. Sorry, were you speaking?—I thought it was the toilet gurgling.

11. Attorneys at dawn

All right, you can have the condo, but I get the CDs. No, not the *recordings*, you idiot, the *money*. Oh yeah?—over my dead body. Whoops, just kidding, Your Honor.

The Songwriter's Love Call

Hello, Mary Lou? . . .

Don't hang up, I just called to say I love you. I can't help myself—I've got to have you back in my arms again. I can't stop loving you, can't get used to losing you. My world is empty without you, babe. I'm all shook up.

Baby, come back. Give me just a little more time, we can work it out. We've only just begun. Love will keep us together, and you can't hurry love. I'm hopelessly devoted to you. You're my everything: You are the sunshine of my life, you are my destiny. You light up my life. You're my dream lover—let me be your teddy bear.

. . . No, I'm all by myself. Lucille? Mandy? Michelle? That'll be the day. I got you, babe, and you're the one I want. It's just the two of us. Don't you want me? I want you to want me. We were so happy together, I can't believe you're leaving me. Where did our love go?

Don't be cruel. Don't go breaking my heart. Do you really want to hurt me? Try a little tenderness. Don't let me be lonely tonight, I've been lonely too long. And you're so far away. Are you lonesome tonight? I'm so lonesome I could cry. Help me make it through the night. I want to hold your hand, I want to make it with you. I'm in the mood for love—I feel like making love—all night long . . .

What d'you mean the thrill is gone? I never promised you a rose garden. Have mercy, baby—let's hang on. I want you. You belong to me, and when a man loves a woman . . .

All right. Let it be. You've lost that loving feeling. I guess it's all over now. No, don't worry, baby—that's life. Que sera, sera. It's just that breaking up is so very hard to do. But remember: you've got a friend—can we still be friends? I'll be there, I'll keep holding on. I wish you love . . .

Bye bye, love.

P.S. I love you.

Sex Guide for Teens

1. Shoot the shit.

2. Get some tongue sushi.

3. Grab ass and feel up.

4. Get nekkid.

5. Wear the raincoat.

6. Parallel park.

7. Bouncy-bouncy.

8. Go over the mountain.

9. Bail, man.

16: Famous Figures in Love Lore

The greatest love is a mother's;
Then comes a dog's;
Then comes a sweetheart's.

—Polish proverb

Aphrodite (Roman name Venus), was the winner of the first beauty contest. Since she was the goddess of beauty and love, runners-up Athena (Wisdom) and Hera (Marriage) felt that choosing her as Miss Greece was a tad unfair. They complained as only angry goddesses can complain and tried to organize a boycott of the Olympics, Greek olives, and feta cheese. In retaliation Aphrodite gave birth to **Eros**, or Cupid, who forever after made people in love lose all their wisdom and want to get married.

Eros later made even more excrement hit the mythical fan by tossing an apple inscribed "for the fairest" toward Juno, Venus, and Minerva, which was really asking for trouble.

Irving Buntz, a shopkeeper in rural Wisconsin in the late 1800s, was the little-known inventor of the pornograph. For centuries before, those who purchased pornography had nothing to play it on. Buntz's invention was very popular at the turn of the century for whiling away the long Upper Midwestern winter nights, but eventually lost out to the proliferation of full-color magazines, and later the VCR and hardcore videotapes. Sadly, despite diligent searches by historians, cultural anthropologists, and antique dealers, no pornographs seem to have survived to this day.

Casanova, the Italian author of the eighteenth century, was more than just a famous lover of women (and possibly anything else that moved). He was also, if not the *inventor* of the condom, its most diligent tester. His version, made from the bladder of a sheep, is credited with decimating half of Europe's flocks of that period and may explain the sudden development of cotton clothing as an alternative to wool. This may also add new meaning to the term "wolf in sheep's clothing."

Cinderella, this teen from the wrong side of the tracks gets dissed by her cruel hosebag stepsisters and stepmom. Cinderella wants to do the club thing and rave all night like everyone else, but she has to stay home and not only clean her *own* room but the rest of the dump too. It was *too* gross. But, like, out of the *sky* just about, comes her Fairy Godmom—no, really—who waves this, like, *magic* wand and gives her *the* most wicked dress. And a rude limo and everything. So when she goes to the rave she's the killingest chick in the room and there's this stud muffin prince and they dance and he falls for her, like, *majorly*. But she has to bail 'cause the rules say she's gotta be home by midnight, can you believe it? Bummer. But this prince guy finds one of Cinderella's Docs or high-tops or something and asks around to see who it fits. 'Course the stepsisters are too, y'know, *huge*, and it turns out that so's the rest of the dames and countesses and stuff. Well, so anyway the prince eventually finds

Cindy at home wearing these really *bald* clothes and with broken nails and her hair all, like, totally *fried*, but he loves her anyway and they go off and I guess she becomes a princess.

So Cinderella's name is used for this *syndrome* thing where babes who've got it are always waiting for their prince to come along and carry them off. Always waiting to be rescued from their bogus lives by some rich dude. Yeah, right. Get *real*. As if *these* days there's gazillions of princes. I mean, prince of *what*, anyway? Some cheesy place with dirt streets and no air conditioning? I'm *sure*.

Coitus Interruptus, a senator in Rome around A.D. 80, is credited with being the first person to practice birth control. It is possible that he discovered his system by accident, since if we read between the lines of his surviving writings we can surmise that he was caught in Flagrante Delicto (a town just outside Pompeii) by his mistress's husband. Whether or not this is true, Coitus has inadvertently given his name to the earliest—and incidentally cheapest—form of contraception.

Mademoiselle Dubois, a French actress of the 1770s, was an insatiable lover and as a result became the unacknowledged originator of "The Love Boat." She kept an accurate account of her sexual alliances, which over twenty years totaled 16,527, an average of two and a half a day. Since she disliked making love with the same man twice, she soon exhausted the supply of attractive men in Paris and its environs. Eventually she was obliged to resort to importing lovers from elsewhere, and her *bateaux d'amour* loaded with eager young men docked daily at Calais.

Ernst Gräfenberg, German gynecologist, discovered what he promptly named the *G-spot*, a place on the upper wall of the vagina that stimulates a particular kind of orgasm in many women. The finding came as quite a surprise to Ernst, and even more so to Mrs. Gräfenberg, who was just looking to kill a few minutes before the store opened.

Herpes, another Greek, was the god of surprise gifts. Originally renowned for the more positive of love presents, he later became careless. His name is now attached, of course, to mementos of a more unwanted nature.

Mona Lisa, or *La Gioconda*, is the name given to the famous portrait by Leonardo da Vinci of the woman with the enigmatic smile. Recent research, largely based on documents in Leonardo's unique reversed handwriting found in an old Florentine church, indicates that she was not his lover, nor even his favorite model, but the woman who delivered his pizza on Tuesdays. He apparently cajoled her into sitting for him when his usual model was indisposed with the hiccups. Mona's absence from her delivery route led to seventeen stone-cold pizzas and her being fired.

The Puritans are not often spoken of in the same breath as love, since they were so down on any free, physical expression of the emotion. But there's nothing like driving something underground to make it popular, and they ensured love's survival by their suppression of it. They of all people should have known men and women will always be attracted to sects. We can thus thank the Puritans for helping to keep love alive through some otherwise strict and humorless times.

Clues to Infidelity

Credit card receipts for double rooms on "business" trips.

Hickeys.

Working late, but not at work.

Strange perfumes.

Sudden, and temporary, increase in sexual appetite.

Sudden, and permanent, decrease in sexual appetite.

Lost underwear.

When you answer, hang-up phone calls.

When your partner answers, many wrong numbers.

Calling out different name at height of passion.

Unaccountable mileage on the car.

Frequent visits to "the dentist," "the doctor," "the library."

III

Relating

The History of Relationships

PREHUMAN

Bump into each other while swinging through trees

Pregnancy

Birth of baby

▼

Baby clings to mother and eventually drops somewhere

STONE AGE

Discover sex by accident

Pregnancy

Share cave

Birth of baby

▼

Eat baby, unless full

IRON AGE

Coupling

Pregnancy

Share hut

Birth of baby

Ignore baby until old enough to work

MEDIEVAL

Attraction

Coupling

Pregnancy

Marriage

Share hovel

Birth of baby

Sell baby

1800s

Attraction

Courtship

Marriage

Share house

Pregnancy

Birth of baby

Leave baby with nurse

1900–1950

Attraction

Courtship

Marriage

Share house

Pregnancy

Birth of baby

Baby and mother stay home for fifteen years

60s & 70s

Attraction

Coupling

Attraction

Coupling

Attraction

Coupling, etc.

1990s

Attraction

Courtship

Coupling

Marriage

Share condo

Pregnancy

Birth of baby

Rent baby for commercials

Sex Guide for Intellectuals

1. Turn conversation to eros and *fin de siècle* libido, ecdysiasis and its endocrinal repercussions, the aphrodisiac qualities manifested by the ingestion of edible marine mollusks of the family *Ostreidae*.
2. Decrease interpersonal distance between oneself and the object of one's amorous intent, triggering pheromone and endorphin production.
3. Osculate.
4. Focus on haptic senses by exploring the tactile qualities of partner's secondary sexual characteristics.
5. Disattach certain critical over- and undergarments, providing adequate state of *déshabillé* and access to pertinent physical accoutrements.
6. Ascertain appropriate placement of prophylactic.
7. Achieve coitus.
8. Initiate rhythmic undulations until *le petit mort* and its concomitant synaptic pyrotechnics is experienced by, hopefully, both.
9. Exchange compliments and other sundry pleasantries until both partners are in the arms of Morpheus.

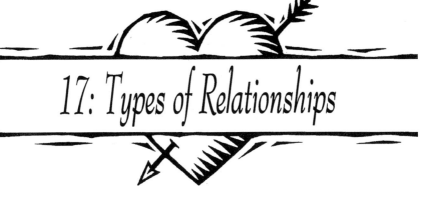

17: Types of Relationships

Platonic love is love from the neck up.
—Thyra Samter Winslow

Adulterous
Could we just *once* meet and *not* make love? You *know* I can't stay the night. No, weekends are out—it's nooners or nothing. I told you—don't call me at home.

Analytical/psychological
I think it's because you have these unresolved feelings toward your father that you won't let me smoke my pipe indoors. I think I've found some of your hidden agendas in the basement, Blanche. Look, sometimes a cigar is just a cigar. Please, Charles, not the dream analysis again—I'm late for work.

Childish/immature
Wanna dwinkie? Wanna do naughty things? Oooh, what's this? Does little Dickie wanna play doctor?

Comedic
Your teeth are like stars—they come out at night. Hey, that reminds me—did I ever tell you the one about the gynecologist? I think I know why you gave your penis a

name, Wayne—it's because you don't like to be bossed around by a stranger.

Controlling
Wipe your feet. I'm not going out with you unless you change those awful clothes. Don't kiss me before you've flossed. No, don't touch me like that—do it like this. Not like that, fool. Did you wash your hands? I may feel like making love at 21:48 on Wednesday, but confirm with me first. You've hung the toiletpaper roll the wrong way again, idiot.

Disposable one-nighters/Kleenex
Did you want any breakfast before you go, uh—don't tell me, uh, *Jane?* . . .

Doormat/masochistic
I detest myself and you seem like just the person to treat me as badly as I deserve, so let's go for it. You want access to my bank account? Sure! Use my credit cards, too. No, that's okay, take my car—I'll take the bus.

Flirtatious
Mmmmm, you look pretty good yourself. How about if we—oh, gotta go. My husband's waving at me.

Female bonding
Did you *see* what she was wearing? Talk about fashion victim. Yeah, that Bill—whew!—what I wouldn't give to find *him* in my stocking on Christmas morning. No, I just get mad enough to chew nails about three days before. Is that water retention, or are you putting on weight? Yeah, mine's not much either—but at least he's straight and single. Is *that* her boyfriend?—I thought she'd brought a Cabbage Patch doll. You should try the Clinique stuff. Hey, let 'em watch the game, who cares?

Male bonding

Nah, Hobson was 31 for 91 which gives him a .341 compared to his .299 in '90, Garcia was 7–4, walked seven and gave up five, but took a 1–0 lead in the seventh, and Snipes's homer broke a 6–6 tie, giving him a 2.16 ERA. Hey, that Henry can drink fourteen bourbons before he talks to Ralph on the white phone — that's my kind of friend, man. I like him so much I could punch his lights out. Yeah, I was three when my paw gave me my first rifle. Hey, Dolores — get me another beer. An' one for my buddy here. Hey, dude, wanna fight?

Mature

You wash, I'll dry; then tomorrow I'll wash and you dry. Hey, we're out of Lemon Joy again. Are you sure this is two-ply? Look, munchkin, I got you a subscription to *Reader's Digest*. I think we need more cruciferous vegetables in our diet. D'you think it's time we replaced our old toothbrushes?

Motherly

Now wrap up warmly. Did you have enough to eat? How about some hot chocolate? You look tired — don't stay up so late. Want me to sew a button on that while you're here? Don't forget your rubbers, now.

Obsessive

If he doesn't call by eight I'm slashing my wrists. If I can't have her then *no one will*. If I camp out here in his backyard he's sure to love me back. If she doesn't stop seeing that creep I'm detonating a small nuclear device in Akron. I'll just hide in his cupboard and surprise him.

Politically correct/radical

Is that teargas in your eyes or are you just pleased to see me? Let's do it on the Trotsky poster. I just love the way you hand out leaflets. Don't you find the Democratic process . . . *exciting?*

Red hot
Couldn't we . . . what about . . . have you ever tried . . . what if we just . . . if you move . . . now if I . . . then . . . aaaaaaaaaaaaooooooooooommmmm-mmfffff.

Romantic
Oh look, he dribbles when he eats soup. She says *"heighth."* Isn't she just darling when she microwaves that awful lean cuisine stuff and calls it making dinner? Isn't he just wonderful the way he revs up his Harley at three A.M. and pisses off all my neighbors?

Sadistic/brutal
Take my knife—please. I'm sorry you've seen me like this, Angela—now I'm going to have to punish you.

Senior
Well, he's still got his teeth—or some of them—somewhere. She walks a mean walker, that Gladys. He doesn't have too many liver spots, and at least they're not malignant. So what if she's a little forgetful—what's worth remembering?

Soulmates
We were lovers in Ancient Greece. The sun rises in your nostrils. The touch of your eyelashes is like the wingbeat of a thousand butterflies. You are my love goddess—I sacrifice myself on the altar of your bellybutton. I worship the hair in your ears. Your neck is like a swan's, and I must kiss your feathers.

Us against the world
My parents will never agree—let's elope to Reno. If they catch us we'll throw ourselves off something, then they'll be sorry. Let's rent *Bonnie and Clyde* again.

Diplomat's Love Letter

My Most Favored Nation—
You have kidnapped my heart and held it hostage. Your glances have targeted my bases, your looks have impacted my soul.

I am adrift in a no-man's-land without hope of rescue. I need your humanitarian aid. I need a Red Cross airlift of your love.

My policy of nonintervention can last no longer. I want to destabilize your government. I want to storm your embassy. I yearn to explore your parameters, undermine your defenses. I'd like to reconnoiter the infrastructure of your private sectors. I dream of involving you in undercover operations.

Can we de-escalate our hostilities, negotiate a truce? Couldn't we at least initiate a feasibility study of a coalition? Peaceful coexistence? Détente? Can we meet for peace talks in some demilitarized zone?

I would never monopolize your affections. I envision no totalitarian regime, no dictatorship. We could achieve a balance of power, I know it.

Are my feelings really unilateral? Anonymous sources suggest otherwise. I know you're not interested in public affairs, public relations, but we can be clandestine; we can keep our actions covert. I can be diplomatic.

Tell me my glasnost has not been a tactical error. Tell me you're nonaligned, open to free trade. Put aside your protectionist policies— throw open your borders and accept my advances.

It would be a liberation, not an invasion. We could live in a new climate of rapprochement. We could reciprocate, become bipartisan. Together we could work toward perestroika. As allies, we could move into the new century in a spirit of unity and cooperation.

Your trading partner

Where the Money Goes

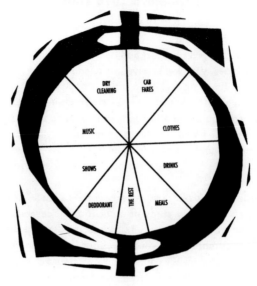

SINGLES

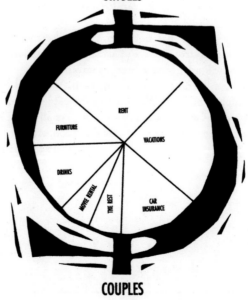

COUPLES

18: The Relationship: One Month, One Year

Let there be spaces in your Togetherness.
—Kahlil Gibran, *The Prophet*

One month	One year
I love his mustache—it's so distinguished.	That stupid brush on his upper lip gives me hives.
Her perfume still lingers on my pillow.	She always wears that insect repellent.
He has such a unique style.	Everything he wears is either ten years out of date or just plain weird.
I love her little inconsistencies—she's so full of surprises.	These mood swings indicate a serious neurosis.

One month	One year
Hands off, girls. He's mine.	Hey, want him? Take him.
She and I have so much in common.	We have absolutely nothing in common.
His snores are so endearing.	He sleeps like a pig.
I can tell when she's turned on by that mischievous, sultry look.	Oh, spare me the coy batting of the eyelashes.
I love the way he looks so rumpled in the morning.	Jesus H. Christ.
What a powerful woman—what a strong personality.	What a hostile bitch.
I'm crazy about the way he tastes when we kiss.	I wish he'd floss more often.
She's such a free spirit, so spontaneous.	What a sociopath.
His little belly is so cute. I'm glad he's not one of those gym jocks.	Don't just sit there, lard-ass. Get some exercise.
What grace, what poise.	Posing again.
What a deliciously craggy face.	His complexion's like the surface of an asteroid.

One month	One year
I just called to say hi, lover.	I just called to say what's your goddamn problem about last night anyway?
He tells such funny stories.	Please, not that one again.
She's so neat.	How anal can you get?
He's so sensitive and caring.	What a wimp. Give me a macho man any day.
He's so strong and masculine.	What a dickhead. Give me a sensitive man any day.
I love it when she wakes me up to make love.	What is it now, for God's sake?

Keys to a Long-lasting Relationship

Lower your expectations.

Don't get together very often.

Buy a punching bag and use it regularly.

Hash out what *has* to be hashed out; let the rest slide
and order a pizza.

Don't work together.

Myopia.

Selective hearing.

Selective memory.

Remember that what pisses you off most about them
is what pisses you off about yourself.

Sign prenuptial agreements.

Remember divorce lawyers' fee scales.

19: Slip Out the Back, Jack:

Frankly, my dear, I don't give a damn.
—Clark Gable in *Gone With the Wind*

We've all faced this difficult situation at one time or another, as dumper and/or dumpee. Here are some handy stock solutions:

Blunt
You're the worst. We're history. We should call it quits.

Cold
All right, that's it. That's the last straw. Get your things out of the bathroom. And don't forget your Abba albums. No, don't look at me with those spaniel eyes—you had your chance. I don't know why I bothered with you at all. What a waste of time. I should charge you for wasted life span. No, leave those—the whips are mine. Don't call, don't write, and never darken my diaphragm again.

Confusing
Darling, it's no use. I've tried, but I'm just not on your level. You're too good for me. I thought I could try to improve, but it's just not working. I know—you've been

patient with me, but this can't continue. I'm no good, never will be. It was kind of you to put up with me this long. I think it's best to make a clean break. Yes, it'll hurt for a while, but I'll get over you. Somehow. In time. Go now, sweetheart, and think of me sometimes, just as I'll have my bittersweet memories of our times together.

Cowardly
Hi, this is Jeannie. I'm not home right now, but leave me a message with your number and I'll call you back soon as I get back from the mall. And if it's Eugene—I'm seeing your best friend Mark, so don't call me anymore. Wait for the beep.

Cowardlier
I just couldn't take it anymore so Im leavin you an the twelve kids an Im takin the station waggen also. Dont try to find me Im going where I will be hapy for once. Thoes twenty yeers we spent togethr was a big misteak an Im goin to start again somewhere else. I have takin all the money. You can get welfair.

Cruel
I'm leaving you for Judd next door. Yes, Judd and I have been mattress dancing behind your back every time you went off to work, Vernon. He's a much better lover than you. What's more he doesn't always leave me with the wet spot. He has a better car than you, too. And more money. And a hot tub. We're going to live in the Caribbean on his island. So there.

Dear John
How are things at the front? The news says there is a darn big ol' ruckus going on over there. I hope you're OK. I am fine. Remember Blaine from the Dairy Queen? We all used to play softball after school? Anyway, Blaine has been very good with Mom and all, and says to say hi. Oh, by the

way, Blaine and me are getting married Saturday at St. Margaret's.

Hysterical
That's IT! I've had ENOUGH! I can't TAKE any more. You drive me CRAZY! Stay AWAY from me! The next time you hear from me it'll be from my LAWYER! No, wait—the next time you hear from my . . . the next person you hear from . . . HOW DARE YOU LAUGH AT ME! I'm LEAVING—you hear me? LEAVING! What? All right, it's my place—so YOU'RE leaving!

Legal
You are herewith ordered to vacate the premises owned by Mr. Heston LeRoy Lockwood and return all gifts and shared possessions, including one red Chevrolet Corvette, license "2MY QTPY," one solitaire diamond and gold engagement ring inscribed "To my Bunny forever, Heston," and one *Miss Piggy's Workout Book,* by or before the thirty-first of this month. Failure to comply with these orders will result in legal action.

Melodramatic
Give me liberty or give me death!

Objective
Sometimes two people who have walked life's path together, side by side, come to a crossroads. And sometimes one direction is good for one person but not for the other. We have come to the intersection of our love, dearest, and I'm not going your way. As a matter of fact, I'm going to Baltimore with Kimberly.

Pedantic
Don't think of it as good-bye, Daphne, but as *au revoir,* which, as you know, means *until we meet again.*[1] Our *divertissement* has been a truly enriching experience, I want

1. When, preferably, hell freezes over.

you to know, and I'm certain we'll have many, many more. It's just that right at this particular moment in time I'd very much enjoy being on the opposite hemisphere of the planet[2] from you, sweetness. Nothing personal, you understand—I'm sure it's just some little *mal de coeur* I'm going through. Nevertheless I do think it wise if we just say ta ta[3] for now.

Poetic

What happened to 8-track tapes, vinyl records, Beta, quadraphonic, black and white TV?

What happened to puka beads, caftans, Nehru jackets, patches?

What happened to VW bugs, leaded gas, MGBs, rotary engines, cheap airfares?

What happened to the Beatles, the Turtles, the metric system, est seminars?

What happened to pet rocks, mood rings, Smurfs, bean bags, and blacklight posters?

What happened to the elastic in my Jockey shorts, and while I'm on the subject, what happened to our love?

Preppie

But Bobby, Daddy says you really aren't going *any*where with that *awful* job of yours. He says you'll never, ever be able to keep poor Buffy in the manner to which she's become accustomed, and I just couldn't *bear* scrimping and saving like your family has done all their squalid little lives. It's just so . . . *gauche*. I mean, I really *do* love you, but *really*, a girl can't be expected to live on no money to speak of. What would they say at the club? Honestly, I don't think it's unreasonable of me to expect a little *more* out of

2. Another continent will suffice.
3. Or cheerio.

112

life. After all, our family did come over on the ship after the ship after the *Mayflower*. The *Julyflower*, I think it was. Anyway, we have a *reputation*, Bobby dear. You *do* understand, don't you? *Do* tell your quaint friends good-bye from me, won't you? Oh, and Daddy says you can keep the golf clubs.

Sarcastic/snide

Thank you for the enlightening education of being in love with you. I had always wondered what it was like to eat broken glass, stick my head into a blast furnace, poke my fingers into a working waste-disposal. Now I never need to experience a hemorrhoidectomy or passing a kidney stone. Thanks to you I needn't wonder what it would be like to have my eyes poked out with shish kebab skewers or be flayed alive with barbed wire. Being involved with you has been one long, fascinating enema, an appendectomy with a rusty steak knife, electroshock therapy. My tooth nerves have been sandpapered with your sentimentality, my toe-nails ripped out with your fondness. But my conscience will no longer allow me to greedily hoard your riches, and I must share them with others. So good-bye, and may God help the rest of the world.

But despite the mental rehearsals, most good-byes end up . . .

Inarticulate

It's no . . . I can't . . . you just . . . why did you have to . . . but it could've, *I* could've been . . . why does it always . . . oh, it's no use . . . it doesn't matter any . . . but why, *why?* I just wish . . . if only we . . . if only you had . . . no, it's not just you, it's just that . . . yes, yes, you're right. I guess so . . . oh, really? Oh yeah? *Oh yeah?* Now wait just a minute . . . What about . . . oh, and I suppose . . . Yeah? Well, *yo' mama.*

Contraceptive Effectiveness

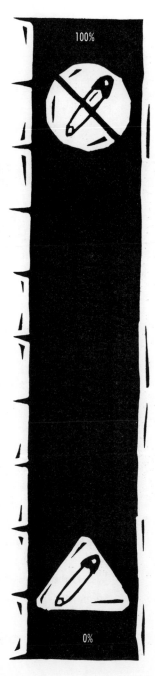

100%

Celibacy
Homosexuality
Implants
Male Sterilization
Female Sterilization
Injectable Progestogen
The Pill
IUD
Condom
Diaphragm
Sponge
Cap
Withdrawal
Periodic Abstinence
Spermicide

Chance

Praying Really Hard

0%

20: Recycling Relationships

Love makes the time pass.
Time makes the love pass.
—French proverb

What to do when sweethearts turn sour.

In these energy-conscious days, when we try in various ways to save and recycle our used items, it's easy to forget our relationships.

What about all that emotion we expended on those loves of the past? What happened to all the passion and energy spent on that affair, that fling, that marriage?

Did we just toss it away when it no longer worked, like a used Kleenex, a disposable razor, a candy wrapper? Did we throw it out and try to forget it ever happened, littering the back alleys of our personal past with the wrecks of intimacy, the dregs of love, the rotting rinds of relationships gone bad?

Do you carry with you a garbage bag full of broken dreams, broken promises? Has your life become a landfill of lost love?

Well, it's time we no longer waste partnerships that

didn't work out—now we can recycle them. Don't just dump the turkey who stood you up twice in a row—sic him on that obnoxious bitch at your health club. Don't just ignore the woman who turned out to be interested in you only for the expensive restaurants she could sucker you into taking her to—introduce her to your boss. They deserve each other.

And what about reusing old relationships? The nice safe guy you dumped for the high-powered asshole who split after three weeks—maybe he's still at his old number. Nice and safe is *fashionable* now, after all. The woman you dropped because she didn't like your friends—maybe she was right. Your buddies *are* rude and flatulent. Call Information, find her, and ask her out again. Why start with stiff and starchy new involvements when you can step back into comfortable, broken-in ones?

Biodegradable is the key word these days, and we've all been in degrading situations at least once. So get together with friends, find out your worst dating experiences, then get those deadly dates together. It's only fair, and it may prevent them from trapping more innocents. Besides, it will clean up our romantic environment.

As for those *extremely* toxic individuals you may have come across—only occasionally, of course—those should be rounded up by the city and placed in a specifically designated dump site where they won't leak into and contaminate other's lives.

The days of wasting our precious natural resources are over. There's only so much love to go around, so it doesn't make sense to use it up indiscriminately and lose it forever, along with the dodo, the passenger pigeon, and the Brazilian rain forests. What if there were a love drought? What if romance had to be rationed? There would be no Valentine's Day, no dozen red roses with baby's breath, no long simpering phone calls in the middle of the night. No sitting on park benches gazing like moonstruck sheep into each other's eyes, no wandering hand in hand with moronic smiles, no lazing around in bed discussing each other's scars. No more goofy love songs, no Barbara Cartland novels, no dimly lit dives with romantic ambience. No "I ♥" bumper stickers. A kind of global cooling. Imagine life with only sitcoms and fast food for fun. Scary, isn't it?

No, let's use our love wisely with our new ecological awareness, and save some for our grandchildren. They're going to need all the help they can get.

Sex Guide for Sixties-revival Hippies

1. Turn on.

2. Check it out.

3. Find out where it's at.

4. Get into each other.

5. Groove.

6. Get down.

7. Get a brand-new bag.

8. Get it on.

9. Do your thing.

10. Blow your mind.

11. Space out.

12. Crash.

The Ten Commandments of Love

I. I am thy Main Squeeze; thou shalt squeeze no others before me.

II. Thou shalt not take the name of thy Squeeze in vain, nor badmouth me behind my back.

III. Remember our Anniversary, and keep it holy. Or else.

IV. Honor *my* mother and father. *Thine* are too damn weird.

V. Thou shalt not kill my love by behaving tackily and making me embarrassed to be seen with thee.

VI. Thou shalt not commit adultery, nor shalt thou even *think* about it if thou knowest what's good for thee.

VII. Thou shalt not steal from my purse/wallet while I am in thy bathroom, nor use my credit cards, nor make long-distance calls from my telephone.

VIII. Thou shalt not talk about our personal problems to our friends.

IX. Thou shalt not covet the higher market price of thy neighbor's house.

X. Thou shalt not covet thy neighbor's Squeeze, nor son or daughter, nor stereo, nor BMW.

21: Test Your Lovability Quotient

> *Basically my wife was immature. I'd be at home in*
> *the bath and she'd come in and sink my boats.*
> —Woody Allen

Are you really equipped to deal with a loving, long-term relationship? Take this simple test and see.

1. **Which of these moves you most?**
   A. a picture of your first love
   B. a picture of your first dog
   C. a pitcher of margaritas

2. **You've just finished making mad, passionate love and you lie beside your lover happily exhausted. Do you:**
   A. compliment him/her on their technique?
   B. ask worriedly if you were good enough?
   C. pay?

3. **You arrive at a party at which you hardly know anyone. Do you:**
   A. look around with self-confidence and pick someone to introduce yourself to?
   B. slink to the stereo and spend the entire evening reading the inserts in the CD boxes?

C. head for the bar and sink as much Dutch courage in as short a space of time as possible, then embarrass yourself and everyone else by involuntarily tossing your tostadas over a priceless antique?

4. **At this party, someone to whom you are *very* attracted comes up to you and expresses interest. Do you:**
   A. chat politely for a while and then suggest you both go somewhere less noisy?
   B. turn purple, sputter something incoherent, and spill the bean dip over him/her?
   C. immediately make an obscene suggestion, accompanied by explanatory gestures just in case it wasn't fully understood?

5. **Still at the same party, someone to whom you are *not* attracted comes up to you and expresses interest. Do you:**
   A. chat politely for a while then excuse yourself?
   B. ask for the location of the restroom and climb out its window, snagging your best pants on the sill?
   C. laugh nastily and say, "In your *dreams*, butt-face!"

6. **You are happily involved with someone, yet you meet another who attracts you equally. Do you:**
   A. ruefully explain that the timing is all wrong?
   B. get his/her number just in case you break up with your current lover soon?
   C. get happily involved with him/her too.

7. **You suspect your lover of seeing someone else. Do you:**
   A. sit him/her down and try to talk it through in a rational and caring way?
   B. wear a false nose and wig and follow him/her around to check on their movements?

C. shower lover with abuse, threaten with various weapons, and throw lover and his/her toiletries out the window?

8. Which of these excites you most?
A. a sexy phone call from your Significant Other at midday, midweek
B. old *National Geographic* pictures of naked primitive tribespeople
C. pickled pig's feet

9. Your lover wants to introduce you to his/her parents. Do you:
A. dress nicely, take a small present and wow them with your charm and wit?
B. break out in blotches, arrive late, and say nothing but laugh at inappropriate times all evening?
C. borrow a full, used Hell's Angels outfit, eat with your fingers, tell off-color jokes to the mother, and try to enlist the father in a belching contest?

10. You are about to go out on a date but an old friend calls and needs help with an emergency. Do you:
A. cancel the date, explain the situation and ask for a rain check?
B. ignore the friend and go, but spend the whole date feeling miserably guilty?
C. adopt an accent, pretend they have a wrong number and hang up?

11. Your lover has had a bad week and arrives looking exhausted. Do you:
A. suggest you call out for Chinese food, and curl up in front of the fire with brandy and massage oil?
B. petulantly accuse him/her of trying to get out of seeing you with the old "I've had a bad week" ploy?

C. ridicule lover for being soft, weak, and lazy, then drag him/her out for a 10k, a dance, and a walk to the top of the tallest local landmark, then get annoyed at him/her for not being more affectionate when you return at 3 A.M.?

12. **Your lover is clearly upset about something. Do you:**
    A. ask what the trouble is and if you can help in any way?
    B. ask what you've done wrong this time and why he/she is always picking on you?
    C. trip lover in the street and give him/her something to *really* whine about?

13. **You and your lover have a disagreement about who does what housework. Do you:**
    A. make a list of what needs to be done and try to divide the duties fairly?
    B. refuse to talk about it, pout, sulk, and leave, slamming the door on your way out?
    C. trash the place and ask what he/she thinks about *that!*

14. **Your lover points out that you could stand to lose a little weight. Do you:**
    A. work out an exercise regimen that you can do together?
    B. burst into tears and console yourself with an entire Sara Lee cheesecake?
    C. scream *"You're* stupid, but at least I can lose weight whenever I feel like it."

15. **Every time you want to make love, your partner complains of a headache, stomachache, or some other ailment. Do you:**
    A. ask if there's a deeper issue that needs to be dealt with?

B. throw a tantrum, accusing your lover of anything and everything that comes into your head?

C. fill the entire bedroom with Excedrin, Pepto-Bismol, Alka-Seltzer, Metamucil, No-Doz, Di-Gel, and Ex-Lax and say he/she doesn't have an excuse anymore?

16. **You meet someone you think is perfect for you and fall immediately in love. This person, however, is indifferent to you. Do you:**
A. chalk it up to experience and move on?

B. pester the person for weeks with phone calls, cards, and unwanted gifts in the desperate hope of changing his/her mind?

C. wheedle person into seeing you just once, keep person waiting so long he/she is sprayed with graffiti by a gang member, then during the date say you find him/her boring and you don't want to see person again?

17. **You're in a relationship that just isn't working. Do you:**
A. discuss parting in as open and nonjudgmental a manner as possible?

B. become more and more obnoxious to be with, pushing your lover away without having to actually deal with the situation directly?

C. pick up someone else and take him/her home, timing your liaison so you'll get caught?

18. **You agree to go on a blind date, and over dinner find yourself repulsed by the other person. Do you:**
A. put on a brave face and try to make it through the evening?

B. phone a buddy and ask him to have you paged to go immediately to the bedside of a dying grandparent?

C. spend the evening leering at others, making insulting personal remarks, and flicking hors d'oeuvres at your partner, then sneak out and stick him/her with the bill?

19. **When you're feeling really affectionate, do you want to:**
    A. shower your lover with kisses and compliments?
    B. shower your lover with abuse for having such low standards as to end up with the likes of you?
    C. shower *with* your lover and several of his/her friends.

20. **When things are going well in your relationship, does it make you want to:**
    A. hold on to the good feelings for as long as possible?
    B. move to another state?
    C. do something disgusting to alienate your lover and show them you're not some sappy, sentimental, limp-wristed wimp.

SCORING

10 for every **A**, *5* for every **B**, and *1* for every **C**.

201+   You cheated. Go wait outside the principal's office.

160–200   You're the perfect lover—compassionate but passionate, sensitive but strong, centered yet outgoing. Your chances of finding an equal are absolutely zero. Your best bet is narcissism. Treat yourself to a good mirror.

100–159   You're definite relationship material: fun but fallible, smart but not smartass. You should have no problem finding and keeping love, and you may want to consider giving seminars in

California to share your skills with others less
well adjusted.

50–99 You're like most people—you like love and
relationships as long as they're easy and fun,
and want out as soon as they're not. Trouble is,
you keep coming up against the same old stuff,
so as long as he/she is clean you might as well
keep the one you've got.

30–49 Well, let's face it, true love never runs smooth,
right? I mean, who wants a relationship to last,
anyway? You might consider therapy to resolve
some problems you still seem to have with your
parents, subliminal self-improvement tapes
playing under the pillow at night, and possibly
an ad in the Personals. Under PETS WANTED.

20–29 Relationships are not exactly your strong
point, are they? Perhaps some social training
would help, starting first with cockroaches,
then hamsters, and progressing slowly over
several fun-filled years to life-sized cardboard
cutouts of humans. You may want to skip the
final stage of getting involved with live people,
if not for your own sake, then for theirs.

0–19 You are an extraterrestrial trying to pass as
human, and it's not working.

The Sailor's Wedding Invitation

Marina Stern and Skip "Skipper" Helms welcome you aboard to join the crew and splice the mainbrace with us as we drop anchor, tie the knot, and become first mates.

At first we were like ships that pass in the night. Because we weren't on the lookout for love and didn't go overboard for each other at first sighting, we gave each other a wide berth. We steered clear of entanglement and let life's winds blow us where they may.

Then we took the wrong tack and drifted off course. We ran afoul of flirtation's flotsam and jetsam, and after cruising aimlessly through a sea of singles became becalmed, adrift. We were out of our depth. The tides of love were at a low ebb, and we ran aground on the shallows of our insincerity. We were left stranded on the shores of loneliness, high and dry.

Little did we know we were in the same boat.

But we weathered the storm, and in its wake we independently chose to take the helm of our life, to be captain of our fate. We suffered a sea change and steered a new course for new horizons; set sail for calmer, clearer waters.

And now we're moored in the Harbor of Happiness.

Reasons Why Relationships End

20% Some silly argument about something totally meaningless that neither partner can even remember after three days.

13% Discovering the other person is not God after all.

12% Tastes, habits, and personalities too dissimilar.

11% Tastes, habits, and personalities too similar.

10% Sexual incompatibility: lack of chemistry.

9% Sexual incompatibility: not agreeing on quantity, quality, or type.

8% Wandering eyes.

7% Wandering other parts.

6% Boredom.

5% Running out of things to say.

4% Interference from partner's parents.

3% Interference from partner's children.

2% Interference from partner's work.

1% Interference on TV/no cable.

22: Love: What It Is?

Love, the quest; marriage, the conquest; divorce, the inquest.
—Helen Rowland

It's not just you and your squeeze that differ on your definitions of love—everyone seems to. The following give some idea of the variation of thought on the subject.

Woody Allen
Love is the answer. But while you're waiting for the answer, sex raises some pretty good questions.

Lynda Barry
Love is an exploding cigar which we willingly smoke.

Ambrose Bierce
Love: a temporary insanity curable by marriage.

Maria Callas
Love is so much better when you're not married.

Robert De Niro (in *Taxi Driver*)
You talkin' to me? You talkin' to *me*?

Lord Dewar
Love is an ocean of emotion entirely surrounded by expenses.

John Dryden
Love's a malady without a cure.

Tamara Freespirit
I always like to think of love as a bridge between souls, you know? A big, beautiful bridge like the Golden Gate that spans the gulf between two people. But it's always being fixed. Those guys with the orange vests are forever patching holes in it and there's those big flashing arrows in the middle of the road and the traffic has to narrow down to one lane and gets all backed up and all the drivers get real hot and angry and end up shouting rude things to each other.

Robert Graves
Love is a universal migraine, a bright stain on the vision, blotting out reason.

Adrian Henri
Love is a fan club with only two fans.

M. Jagger/K. Richards
Love is a bitch.

Jerome K. Jerome
Love is like the measles; we all have to go through it.

Franklin P. Jones
Love doesn't make the world go 'round. Love is what makes the ride worthwhile.

Lennon/McCartney
Love is all you need.

W. Somerset Maugham
Love is what happens to men and women who don't know each other.

Joseph Mayer

A mutual admiration society consisting of but two members. Of these, the one whose love is less intense will become president.

Ryan O'Neill (in *Love Story*)

Love means never having to say you're sorry.

Ovid

A kind of warfare.

Johnny Rotten

Love is two minutes fifty-two seconds of squishing noises.

Roxanne Rottweiler

Love is the raisins in my oatmeal, the cream cheese on my bagel, the whipped cream on my pie. No wonder I can never lose weight.

Helen Rowland

Love: woman's eternal spring and man's eternal fall.

William Shakespeare

Love looks not with the eyes, but with the mind/and therefore is wing'd Cupid painted blind.

Stephen Stills

Love the one you're with.

Lily Tomlin

If love is the answer, could you rephrase the question?

Paul Jean Toulet

Love is those shabby hotels in which all the luxury is in the lobby.

Tina Turner

What's love got to do with it?

Judith Viorst
Love is the same as like, except you feel sexier. And more romantic. And also more annoyed when he talks with his mouth full. And you also resent it more when he interrupts you. And you respect him less when he shows any weakness. And furthermore, when you ask him to pick you up at the airport and he tells you he can't do it because he's busy, it's only when you love him that you hate him.

William "Beanie" Wanamaker
Love is like being whacked behind the ear with a baseball bat, man. An' *I* should know.

Mae West
Love conquers all things except poverty and toothache.

Oscar Wilde
A mutual misunderstanding.

Tennessee Williams
Just another four-letter word.

Butch Yobkovitch
Love is, like, the Vaseline of life. Know what I mean?

And what some of the great minds might've said, had we gotten to them in time:

St. Augustine
Love is made by good and bad demons inside the body. The good demons are doing the work of God in bringing His voice to us; the bad are doing the work of Satan by tempting us to base acts of immorality and sin. The former are the carriers of pure, spiritual love; the latter of all the fun stuff.

St. Thomas Aquinas
Being in love is the highest of human emotions, there-fore it is the closest we come to God, therefore when you're

in love you shouldn't dick around with it or you may not get to heaven.

Cleopatra
Love is just a pain in the asp.

Darwin
Love is Nature's crafty way of assuring the species is perpetuated. Sort of survival of the prettiest.

Edison
Love is one percent infatuation and ninety-nine percent aggravation.

Freud
Love is the embarrassed ego's nice explanation of the id's animal desire for sex.

Hegel
Love is a focus of the ongoing cosmic evolution toward Absolute Spirit and God; those in love are participating in the dialectic of this flow. Another Absolute Spirit, anyone?

Jung
Love is the Mystic Power of the Soul, the Magical Source of the Spirit, an archetypal myth of the collective unconscious. At least, love's been a bit of a myth in *my* life lately.

Kierkegaard
Love is a careless glance from God. By mistake.

Machiavelli
Love is simply a way of getting things out of people. If you want sex, money, gifts, or to be kept comfortably, manipulate someone into falling in love with you. Then they *want* to do things for you, and you don't have to pay them.

Marx
Love is the opiate of the people . . . or was that religion? Oh well, whatever.

Mao Tse-Tung

Love is an imperialist plot to undermine the right-thinking socialistic cooperation of the masses and turn them into lickspittle lackeys of a corrupt capitalism.

Newton

The force of love attraction between any two bodies will be directly proportionate to their unavailability, and inversely proportionate to their suitability for each other.

Nietzsche

Love is an unconscious human drive toward asserting power over others, an attempt to control them with bonds of emotion, to try to bend them with the will into the desired object, to *force* them into submission with—oh, sorry. Got a little carried away for a moment there.

Pavlov

Love is simply a conditioned reaction to something or someone we are attracted to. One of those bells that now and then rings.

Andy Warhol

In the future, everyone will be in love for fifteen minutes.

Sex Guide for Realtors

1. Survey and assessment.

2. Positive appraisal.

3. Determine undivided interest.

4. Make offer.

5. Dispense with encumbrances.

6. Establish common area.

7. Verify adequate insurance coverage.

8. Provided easement.

9. Occupy premises.

10. Exchange deed.

11. Calculate appreciation.

12. Vacate.

Reasons for Marrying:
Putting on the Wedlock

GOOD

Because you can't possibly go on living another day without sharing wedded bliss with this person.

Because her father will blow your goddamn head off with his Remington 870 riot model shotgun if you don't.

MEDIOCRE

Because it seemed like a good idea at the time.

Because everyone does, don't they?

Because he/she has lots of money for you to wallow in.

Because you're tried of looking for sex every night.

Because you'd like a lot of gifts like fondue sets, heavy silverware, and Cuisinart accessories.

So you won't have to feel embarrassed every time you stay over at your partner's parents' house and want to share a room.

Because the relationship isn't going anywhere otherwise, and it's time for either *pro*posal or *dis*posal.

So your kids won't be confused as to their last name.

Because your mother's always been dead set on throwing this spectacular, three-ring circus of a white wedding bash, inviting everyone she's ever known and wanted to impress, with choice of salmon or steak sit-down with maids and butlers and ushers and the whole nine yards, and you don't have the *cojones* to tell her no.

BAD

Because you need someone to cook, clean, and wash and you can't afford a servant.

Because Mom and Dad won't get off your case about wanting some grandchildren to spoil.

Because time is slipping by and you're not getting any younger.

Because it'll be cheaper to live together and share everything.

Because he/she paid you to get a green card.

Because that old biological clock is ticking away and the alarm's about to go off.

Because he/she has a lot of property you can divide when you get divorced next month.

Because she won't sleep with you until you do.

Because your class reunion's coming up and you were voted least likely to marry.

Because this way it's easier to get the in-laws to baby-sit.

Some Side Effects of Love

THE MEETING . . .

CLOUD NINE SYNDROME

BOINK-O-RAMA

CLOWNISM

ABSORPTION

DE-PEDESTALIZATION

WAR ZONE

CONSPICUOUS CONSUMPTION

TAMING OF THE SHREW, PART II

SLUGDOM

MULTIPLICATION

BLISSVILLE

23: Alternative Wedding Ceremonies

A man in love is incomplete until he has married.
Then he's finished.

—Zsa Zsa Gabor

Cynical

Well, we all know getting married in these times is at best an anachronism and at worst just plain naive. Why, people who think that signing some paper will actually make a difference need to get their heads examined. Chances are they'll be divorced within six years, or in this state, three, so is it really worth the trouble? Nevertheless these two saps have decided to make the same old mistake and spend the rest of their lies—uh, *lives*—together, and I think they deserve our support for trying. Gotta keep the lawyers in business after all, right? So—and don't say I didn't warn you—I pronounce you future ex-husband and ex-wife.

New Age

We are gathered here today to share the joining of two spirits on this earthly plane. Their enlightened consciousness has drawn them together to interweave their souls on a karmic level. Their higher selves have aligned to experience the divine energy manifested by love. Psychically channeled by the cosmos, they met and opened their minds, hearts, and their other chakras to one another until, today, they have achieved oneness. Now, empowering their personal altar with this mutual acceptance of a higher divine mandate over their lives, they align themselves in this timeless transformational dance.

You may now throw organic brown rice and Bach flower remedies.

Punk

You two have, like, decided to, er, ball an' chain it, y'know? To shack in one place, together, sort of. To share stuff, do the livin' together thing. Have babies, who knows? Hey, sorry, man. But, like, we're all here today to see it happen. So now you two are, like, *man*, man, and *wife*, man. Y'know? May the rest of your lives together be cool. But hot, too, know what I mean? I mean, stay cool but don' lose the, uh, whatever that got you together to begin with. See? Shit, you know what I'm talking about. So go forth and, like, *do* it.

Senior

Those who think youth is wasted on the young should be happy for this particular bride and groom. While definitely no longer young—neither of them looks to me likely to see seventy again—they have retained for themselves one of the privileges of youth: young love. Of course, they won't have much time to enjoy it, but hey—they probably don't have the energy to do much anyway. We've all heard of May-September relationships—this is December-December. Still, I'm sure you'll all join with me in hoping they get a good year or two more out of this marriage, otherwise today's going to be a real big waste of time. You caterers better get your invoices in quickly.

145

Yuppie

Dearly Beloved, we are gathered here today to witness these two young, upwardly mobile urban professionals timeshare.

Will you, Bree, drive a Volvo station wagon with car phone, wear Laura Ashley prints, a Piaget watch, Hermès scarves, Ferragamo pumps, and be the perfect mother as well as the perfect executive?

Will you, Dirk, drive a Saab with tinted windows and car phone, wear Giorgio Armani suits, a Rolex, Italian loafers without socks, Cardin sunglasses, and always have immaculate hair?

Do you both promise to live in a gentrified neighborhood with a Soloflex machine, a really expensive stereo system, Gucci luggage? Do you promise to be on first-name terms with your maître d', graze on goat cheese, radicchio, arugula, and shiitake mushrooms, drink caffé lattes and imported mineral waters? Will you collect art and research your family trees?

Do you promise to pre-enroll your future gifted children in a private preschool, subscribe to a diaper service, outfit them in Baby Guess, train them with flashcards? Do you promise to save them quality time, and still be there for each other as long as you both decide the relationship is mutually beneficial?

Then I now pronounce you partners in the firm of Bree and Dirk, and may your stock always go up in value.

24: Romeo and Juliet Get Middle-Aged

*God, for two people to be able to live together for the
rest of their lives is almost unnatural.*

—Jane Fonda

Still star-cross'd after all these years.

SCENE 1, *the Kitchen.*
[JULIET *is at the sink. Enter* ROMEO.]

Juliet: 'Twas quite a number of cups thou sank
Last night, Husband. Dost thou need such an abundance
Of forgetfulness in these meager days of yours?
Romeo: O not again, woman. Get thee off this subject.
'Twas but a party, and I did but party down.
Juliet: Mayhap thy marriage is become burdensome
Of late. Mayhap thou would'st prefer yon Tiffany
Of the bulging bodice—
ROMEO: Tiffany, is it? Thou may'st talk.
What then of Chuck of the swollen biceps?
Methinks my Juliet fawns upon the flexing of his thews
Like a schoolgirl at a wrestling match.
Juliet: Chuck meaneth naught to me; thou know'st.

'Twas just to draw thee from thy infidelities
That I did list to his jokes and laugh a little.

Romeo: Laugh a little! Why, I was afright your face
Might split in twain, your cackle rent the air so.

Juliet: Better a laugh than the copping of a feel
In the kitchen. Dids't think thou were not seen?

Romeo [looking up]: O, that Friar Laurence's potion
Had but work'd to its full, and I been consign'd
To Heaven's bachelor peace; not this,
This souring of sweetness like milk o'erripe,
This hell on Earth, this—

Juliet [gazing out window]: And I had married Paris.
He that seem'd then such slime hath now
Much lands, and vineyards full and ripe—

Romeo: And ducats by the wagonload.

Juliet: And ducats by the wagonload, aye.
It galls me much that had I but wed as my parents' wish
I should now be deck'd in ermine, gold—

Romeo: Soft, woman, or thou shalt be deck'd
By yon well-clenchèd fist—

Juliet: Aye, 'tis oft thy answer to thy vexations,
To threaten me thus with bodily harm
Like the bully who resorts to fisticuffs because
His wits lack requisite pow'r.

Romeo: Aaagh. Thy nagsome tongue doth drive me to't.
It is enough to make St. Francis murder babes.
I was once mild-manner'd, gentle, a dew-eyed lad,
But now thy shrewish whine doth fray my ears
As a dog worries a rag, and, like a dog
I change from lick to bite in my agitation.

Juliet: I worry, true, but not at a rag:
I fret that my erstwhile soft-cheek'd suitor,
Who once said I teach the torches to burn bright,
Now attends to other flames; now spends his eves
At tankard's rim, awash not in passion but ale.

Romeo: Cannot a man have some little fun?
Is being wed a ball blacksmith'd to leg
To circumscribe a bridegroom's movements
In ever-smaller arcs?

Juliet: 'Tis I whose gait hath been curtail'd.
I whose future once was bright with hope,
With honor, with family pride, but I relinquish'd
My noble name to wed a base-born Montague, a fool.

Romeo: Aye, a fool. A fool who could have had
The hand and heart of ev'ry girl in Verona,
Let alone their—

Juliet: Say not this next part, husband,
Or thou shalt hear naught else but from my Lawy'r.

Romeo: 'Tis a voice I would welcome, ere I hear
The voice of Madness within. Rather dead Love's attorney
Than thy morning bickerings—

        [*Enter* STEVE, *clutching books*]

Steve: Mama! Papa! Clamor not at each other again
Today: these razor'd words doth squinch my innards,
And me with a Physicks test at school . . .

Romeo [Aside]: And here be another voice
I should not miss.

Juliet: Sit thee down, Steve, and fasten thy chops
Around your breakfast. Thou needest thy strength.

Steve: I liketh not this seeds and grain,
This paltry mash of goat fodder, this—

Romeo: Eat they food, ungrateful wretch.
I'm in no mood to listen to thy bleatings, and besides,
Think of the less fortunate children in Cathay.
This disrespect is doubtless gain'd from thy mother,
Who, like all the Capulets, worry their men
To early graves, thence live like Queens on their spoils,
While their boy brats grow to make the same mistake.

Juliet: And hast thou finish'd thy petty speech?
What respect is a father owed who works but seldom;

Who hangs at yonder square with his deadbeat friends?
No wonder that the child learns ill at school,
Lags behind his class in Mathematicks:
'Tis from his father's mold he springs.

Romeo: 'Twas not from my mold he sprang, but from
That woeful day when, awaken'd from our druggèd sleeps
By antidotes administer'd at the eleventh hour
We did what lovers do to celebrate their love,
And which old Nature bade us do.

Steve: And what was that, Papa?

Juliet: Never you mind, young man. Your father
Reminisces on things long gone; on days when,
Like a young ram, he acted upon youth's edict.
When his blood sang in his heart and he loved
A young maid right well with't.

Romeo: Oh? And is the ram so old his blood
Hath lost its voice? And doth not the ewe still value
The curl of his horn, albeit gray-nested?

Steve: Rams? Ewes? Horns? Nests?
What means this barnyard of terms? Have I not
Enough schooling without the study of animals
At my morning meal?

Juliet: Finish thy milk and hie thee hence.

[STEVE *Exits*]

Romeo: Aye, thy mother and I have Biology to discuss.

Juliet: Mayhap we, being past the first blush,
Are likewise beyond youth's blushing exercise.

Romeo: Think thou that I am too old to climb thy
Balcony? 'Tis true I am not as spright or limber,
But age hath yet its tenacity; a lad's attentions wander.

Juliet: And I may no longer be east's morning sun,
Nor yet my cheek so bright it shames the stars,
But scale these faded walls again, and steal once more
The fruit of my father's orchard.

Romeo: Ah, now thou talks't fair, fair pet,

For I yet within thee see the maid who stole my heart . . .
    Juliet: And I the callow youth who captur'd mine,
Just thinly cloak'd with time and cares . . .
    Romeo: Still lovely, still my sweet Juliet . . .
    Juliet: And thou, my sweetest Romeo.

[Exeunt upstairs]

Sex Guide for Parents

1. Turn off intercom in baby's nursery; nail child's door closed; change locks on front door once teen has left.
2. Lock selves in bedroom with DISTURB AND DIE sign on doorknob.
3. Try to remember what it was like before you became parents.
4. Attempt to forget offspring's diapers/formula/bedwetting/teething/difficult phase/school bills/school grades/clothes bills/substance abuse/attitude/room state/hairstyle/lifestyle/choice of friends.
5. Turn up easy listening station to tune out offspring's crying/wailing/cursing/guilt trips/threats/thrash rock.
6. Try to forget that lovemaking was what got you into this mess to begin with.
7. Fall asleep from unaccustomed opportunity to relax in peace and quiet.

Divorce Invoice

*Save time settling up at the **end** of your relationship by making a list of expenses **during** it. When the billing and cooing degenerates into just billing, use this handy form to itemize your expenditures. Then simply give to your lawyer or father-in-law.*

	$ Amt.
Staying at hotels/motels/with friends after arguments	_____
Chiropractic treatments after sleeping on sofa	_____
Therapy to restore undermined self-esteem	_____
Mental anguish, general compensation	_____
Therapy to overcome mental anguish	_____
Pain and suffering, general compensation	_____
Extended stay at retreat to overcome pain and suffering	_____
Collagen injections at sites of stress-related wrinkles	_____
Lunches/benders with friends for sympathy	_____
Time lost in career advancement from marital disruptions	_____
Half of house, furniture, cars, bank accounts, etc.	_____
Half of children, if any	_____
Half of your income for the rest of your goddamn life, you bastard	_____
Changing locks, phone number, name, etc.	_____
Replacement of limited edition Elvis Presley plate	_____
Removal of fragments of Elvis plate from buttocks	_____
Total $	_____

Postscript

Teleprompter for Married Couples

DON'T YOU TAKE THAT TONE WITH ME I DON'T HAVE TO LISTEN TO THIS WHO DO YOU THINK YOU ARE ANYWAY GOD'S GIFT TO MEN/WOMEN WHO DO YOU THINK I AM ANYWAY PICK UP YOUR OWN SOCKS THAT'S RIGHT LEAVE SEE IF I CARE YOU THINK YOU'RE SO CLEVER I'LL NEVER KNOW WHAT I SAW IN YOU NOBODY WOULD PUT UP WITH THIS KIND OF TREATMENT YOU USED TO BE SO CONSIDERATE NOW I'M JUST YOUR DOORMAT PUT DOWN THAT REMOTE AND LISTEN JUST ONCE I'D LIKE TO . . .